UNITY THROUGH
Repentance

UNITY THROUGH
Repentance

The Journey to Wittenberg 2017

THOMAS COGDELL WITH AMY COGDELL

Available at missionbooks.org

Unity through Repentance: The Journey to Wittenberg 2017

Published by William Carey Publishing
10 W. Dry Creek Cir
Littleton, CO 80120 | www.missionbooks.org

William Carey Publishing is a ministry of Frontier Ventures
Pasadena, CA | www.frontierventures.org

Cover and Interior Designer: Mike Riester
Front cover door image: Jason Peters, Pearpod Design

Photography / Artwork: Thomas Cogdell, Andrew Zimmerman, Christina Cogdell, Dan and Joann Davis, David and Kathi Peters, Franz Rathmair, Jo Hoffman, Julia Stone, Noah Cogdell, Ryan and Noleen Thurman, Verena Lang, James B. Janknegt, Rebekah/Sarah Brydon

ISBNs: 978-1-64508-311-5 (paperback), 978-1-64508-313-9 (epub)

Printed Worldwide

26 25 24 23 22   1 2 3 4 5   IN

Library of Congress Control Number: 2022937742

Dedicated to
George and Hanna Miley
and
Hans-Peter and Verena Lang

Contents

Cast of Characters

Many folks contributed in a significant way to Wittenberg 2017! To make it easier for you to keep track of them, I created this list of every person who appears in multiple chapters of the book, with their place of residence.[1]

FRIEDRICH ASCHOFF	German Lutheran, Germany (Klosterlechfeld)
LUDWIG & CECILY BENECKE	German Lutheran / Catholic, Germany (Trieb)
BENJAMIN BERGER	American Messianic Jew, Israel (Jerusalem)
BR. PIETRO BERGERHOFER	German Catholic, Germany (Darmstadt)
KEITH BLANK	American Mennonite, USA (Pennsylvania)
JOHN & ANN † (deceased) 2017 COGDELL	American Anglican, USA (Texas) / heaven
DAN DAVIS	American nondenominational, USA (Washington)
JOHN DAWSON	New Zealander Evangelical, USA (California)
JOCHEN & MIRIAM DEBUS	German Lutheran, Germany (Eimeldingen)
HENNING DOBERS	German Lutheran, Germany (Hannoversch Münden)
FRANZISKUS EISENBACH	German Catholic, Germany (Bad Wimpfen)
JOHANNES FICHTENBAUER	Austrian Catholic, Austria (Vienna)
BEN GIROD	American Amish, USA (Wyoming)
MARIANNA GOL	Russian Messianic Jew, Israel (Beersheba)
RICHARD HARVEY	English Messianic Jew, England (London)
FATHER PETER HOCKEN † 2017	English Catholic, Austria (Hainburg) / heaven
LLOYD HOOVER	American Mennonite, USA (Pennsylvania)
BURKARD HOTZ	German Lutheran, Germany (Darmstadt)
JAYSON KNOX	American nondenominational, USA (Texas)

---

1 Of course, there are many others who appear in only one chapter, and so many more who regrettably couldn't be included by name in this book because of the need to keep it reasonably short. But don't be disappointed if you don't find your name here—you are not forgotten!

SISTER JOELA KRÜGER	German Lutheran, Germany (Darmstadt)
HANS-PETER & VERENA LANG	Austrian Catholic, Austria (Wieselburg)
FATHER LARRY MATTINGLY † 2015	American Catholic, USA (Texas) / heaven
MICHAEL & JOELENE MICHEL	American nondenominational, USA (Texas)
GEORGE & HANNA MILEY	American / German Anglican / Messianic Jew, USA (Arizona)
PHILLIP & CAROLINE OWENS	American Catholic, USA (Texas)
SANDI PEDROTTI	American nondenominational, USA (Texas)
FRANZ RATHMAIR	Austrian Anabaptist / Pentecostal, Austria (Steyr)
PRINCE MICHAEL & PRINCESS PHILIPPA SALM	German Catholic / Lutheran, Germany (Walhausen)
DAVID & GREETJE SANDERS	English / Dutch nondenominational, Germany (Berlin)
HANS SCHOLZ	German Lutheran, Germany (Straubenhardt)
CARDINAL CHRISTOPH SCHÖNBORN	Czech Catholic, Austria (Vienna)
GABRIELA SCHUBERT	Austrian Catholic, Austria (Vienna)
JULIA STONE	English Messianic Jew / nondenominational, Germany (Berlin)
RYAN THURMAN	American Anglican, USA (Arizona)
FATHER DRTAD UZUNYAN	Armenian Eastern Orthodox, Turkey (Istanbul)
HANS WIEDENMANN	German Lutheran, Germany (Königswinter-Oberpleis)
CHRIS & BEA ZIMMERMAN	American Bruderhof, USA (New York)

Foreword

By Father Peter Hocken † 2017

Father Peter Hocken was an English Catholic priest who was at home equally in Mass at the Vatican, a wild Pentecostal service in a warehouse in Los Angeles, or a Messianic Jewish synagogue in Jerusalem. His sharp memory and deep scholarship have contributed immensely to the cause of reconciliation and unity in the body of Christ. He died on June 10, 2017, before the final gathering of Wittenberg 2017 and of course before I began work on this book. Although my desire to have him write the foreword was an impossibility, Father Peter did speak about Wittenberg 2017 in our gathering in 2016. So I took the liberty of asking Mysterium Christi, the Austrian ministry to whom he left stewardship of his legacy, if I could adopt his words into a foreword for this book. They graciously gave me permission to do so, for which I am grateful.

—THOMAS COGDELL

Wittenberg 2017, as an initiative of the Holy Spirit, will be distinguished from all the other events taking place in Wittenberg next year. I think we need to make sure that this initiative is moving forward in the Holy Spirit, through the power of the Holy Spirit, and by the leading of the Holy Spirit.

This is what is special about Wittenberg 2017. I think this puts a particular responsibility on us.

See, I think the whole charismatic movement and Holy Spirit renewal has been hugely important in God's purposes. We often "draw back" from making big claims. On the one hand, that's good, because big claims can just come out of arrogance—thinking how important we are. On the other hand, when we look at what's happened in the world of Christianity in the last one hundred years, we have to see that there is a huge importance in the whole Pentecostal and charismatic movements. And we mustn't sell God short just because of criticism from other people who don't like it.

I think what has happened through this Pentecostal and charismatic working of the Spirit is that we are enabled to recognize fellow believers as equally gifted—people from all kinds of other churches and confessions and streams. It enables us to worship together, to hear the Lord together, to respond to the Lord together, to serve together in a way that was not possible before.

> See, as a charismatic initiative, we can follow God's order—the order of the Holy Spirit.

See, as a charismatic initiative, we can follow God's order—the order of the Holy Spirit. I think God's order normally starts with the charismatic, the creative work of the Spirit. Everything has to start with the creative work of the Spirit. It says in Genesis 1:1–2,

> In the beginning, God created the heavens and the earth.
> Now the earth was formless and empty, darkness was over the surface of the deep, and the Spirit of God was hovering over the waters.

It's like there's an initial chaos and the Spirit hovers over this. This hovering image can be likened to a bird, like a mother with her chicks. I think that this comes first.

And then order begins to form, and things come into harmony, and an element of structure is created.

And so the creative act—and I link this to the charismatic—comes first. And the ordering comes second, and structure.

For example, in the Catholic Church ... often the impression is given that the structure comes first and then you find a place for the charismatic. Father Raniero Cantalamessa was the first person I heard say that the charismatic comes first and then the Spirit does the ordering afterward.[2] He made the point that the charismatic comes first, the Spirit comes first, the creator Spirit, and then the ordering and structuring is also work of the Spirit.

This helps us not to be drawn into the mistake of opposing structure and spirit.

---

2 Father Peter notes that he heard this from Cantalamessa in 1991, at a conference of charismatic Christians in Brighton, England (Father Peter's hometown).

If you look in the history of Israel, you see this—the call of Abraham, and then reflection and understanding develops later.

You see it very clearly in the New Testament. First the event—the event of the incarnation, the event of Jesus calling the twelve, the event of his death, the event of his resurrection, the event of Pentecost. The events come. Then you get the formulation of a message or an understanding of the event—like in 1 Corinthians 15 at the beginning, or in Romans 4:25. So I think theology, the formulation of doctrine, comes later. There's a process here.

> First, the work of the Spirit enables us to know our unity, and then we have to start to think through what this means in terms of our received teachings.

I am really displeased with people who have no time for the ecumenical movement of the twentieth century. This has been really key, even though it suffers from a number of faults. For example, the Gemeinsame Erklärung, or Joint Declaration on Justification by Faith, was the fruit of years of work within the Faith and Order part of the ecumenical movement. This aspect of the ecumenical movement seems to have begun with theologians going back and studying what happened—looking at the development of Lutheran teaching and Catholic teaching (often in response to each other), looking for convergence or clarity and so on. But this is starting at the other end from how things began. First, the work of the Spirit enables us to know our unity, and then we have to start to think through what this means in terms of our received teachings.

This is why this initiative for next year is so important—because it's beginning in God's order: the event comes first, which is outpouring of the Spirit.

But this then has to lead to reflection and teaching.

It doesn't mean there's no theological work [for us] to do—that would be naive. But it does show the unique opportunity this kind of initiative has to achieve—before next year, and afterward as well.

You see, any Christian activity without the Holy Spirit—or trying to be faithful Christians without understanding the role of the Spirit, the creative role of the Spirit—leads to a church focused on the past: "Maintaining our tradition," maintaining the purity of our teaching, and so on. It has little vision. Now it is true that God tells the Israelites to remember everything.

We have to remember the events, the founding events. We also have to remember the promises, which lead us into God's future. Holy Spirit renewal will always produce all of these elements:

No leaving behind of the past,
no disrespect for the past,
but oriented toward future and fulfillment.

This is what the encounter with Israel helps to correct for us, because we have been accustomed to the Jews as a people to whom the promises were given (as Paul says in Romans 9). So that when we meet Messianic Jews, they bring right up the promises given to Israel, and the fulfillment of these promises becomes central. Whereas for a lot of Christians, the promises are more like an appendix on the end, that you occasionally look at. This is just inadequate.

So through the Holy Spirit's work in us, especially for repentance, we can celebrate the 500th anniversary in unity. I think this is maybe where the breakthrough is located, that we will be able to celebrate it in real unity of spirit in the bond of peace—thanking the Lord in unity, grieving before the Lord in unity, with a shared vision and a common hope. It doesn't mean that differences between Catholics and Lutherans don't mean anything anymore. There is unfinished business, but the Holy Spirit enables us to be one in these things so that we can worship

> So through the Holy Spirit's work in us, especially for repentance, we can celebrate the 500th anniversary in unity.

together, proclaim together, and serve together. I think what the Holy Spirit does ... the Holy Spirit doesn't really remove our identities or our confessional identity—it purifies them and it uplifts the basic identity being Christian. Then our confessional church identities are rightly situated within the deepest identity of being Christian and—related to being Christian—being a human being.

We all recognize we need more healing in these identities. But you know, when we gather together here next year in this initiative, we will not be thinking something like "Oh, we're a Catholic delegation taking part in this Lutheran celebration"—not that we're condemning the others who are coming together in this way. And we won't be thinking, "I'm a Catholic and I'm different from them, but we're still able to pray together" or anything like that. We will be united as Christians and as believers in Yeshua. We will be united in these things. That means we will not be above all conscious of the things that have divided, or of our confessional identity—though we're not denying these, and we're not saying they don't matter anymore, because there are further riches the Lord wants to bring together. It's the Holy Spirit that has been poured out in this movement that makes this possible, and we need to fully enter into that and realize what an amazing thing this is.

So as I was led during these days more and more to the role of the Holy Spirit, I think this is where it ends up:

This initiative has to be totally prepared in the Holy Spirit.

And this must be without any boasting, without us making any claims at all or thinking we're especially important. There has to be a radical humility in this—because the movements of the Spirit, well … we have a lot of our own scandals. So it has to be very humble.

But I think we have to take hold of what the Holy Spirit is making possible, through this outpouring in the twentieth and twenty-first centuries.

Thank you very much.

Use the QR code or visit **https://bit.ly/w17fore** to listen to all of Father Peter's talk in 2016, from which this foreword was drawn.

Preface

Wittenberg 2017 is a story of a person. A simple parable may help explain this.

Imagine a father with a child—a daughter. He is the rare combination of wealthy and good-hearted. The girl is four or five years old, which is old enough to know what she wants. What she wants is a Playmobil dollhouse for her birthday. "Daddy, I want a Playmobil dollhouse for my birthday. Please …?"

What is the response of the father?

Next imagine them some years later. The daughter approaches her father with a more sophisticated request. "Dad, I've been noticing a boy in my class at school, who seems lonely. Nobody talks to him. I found out his birthday is just a few days from mine. Can we have a joint birthday party, so that he will have lots of friends and presents? Please …?"

What is the response of the father?

Once again, let your imagination leap forward a few years. The girl has become a young woman, and her father is beginning to gray. She approaches him with a new request. "Father, I've been reading back through your old journals—sorry about that, but you do just leave them laying around. I read where you wrote, that you had always dreamed of visiting the Grand Canyon, but never found the time to go. And, well, my 18th birthday is coming up, and you had asked me what special party I might want, and, well, I wondered, could you and I maybe go to the Grand Canyon together? Please …?"

What is the response of the father?

We must use our imagination one last time, though the scene is more difficult. The daughter, a mature woman now, has contracted a fatal illness, and only has a few months to live. She comes to her father, who is consumed by the cruel prospect of burying his own child. "I have only one request left," she says: "_____? Please …?"

Does it matter what she asks for? Whatever it is, you know the father's response. That man will move heaven and earth to grant his beloved child's final request.

The New Testament reveals to us that God, the singular Creator of the universe, is somehow also three distinct Persons. God is the Father; God is Jesus, the Father's only begotten Son; God is the Holy Spirit, sent by the Father at the Son's request. God has always had relationship within himself, unity within the Trinity.

We also learn from these writings that our earthly relationships at their best provide a faint and blurry picture of the glory of the relationships within the Trinity. Jesus teaches us, "So then if earthly fathers—who have evil in their hearts—give good gifts to their children, how much more will the Father in heaven give the Holy Spirit to those who ask him!" (Luke 11:13)

And we learn in the Gospel of John that Jesus, the only begotten Son of God, actually made a last request of his Father in heaven!

On the night that he faced arrest and imminent crucifixion, Jesus prayed for his disciples. "I pray for them." (John 17:9) They didn't know that they needed prayer. Jesus knew that they needed prayer.

And then Jesus turns his attention to us. "I pray not for my disciples alone. I pray also for whoever will believe in me through their message ..." (John 17:20). Do we know that we need prayer? Perhaps not ... but Jesus knew. He still knows, and "he always lives to intercede ..." (Heb 7:25).

What did Jesus pray for us?

He could have prayed for anything.

He could have prayed for his followers through the ages to be strong in faith ... or to diligently obey his commandments ... or to always serve the poor ... or to maintain correct doctrine ... or to be morally pure ... or to worship in spirit and in truth. All of these are good and right, and were taught by Jesus. He cares about all of these things. But none of them enter into his prayer.

What did Jesus pray for us?

"… that they all will be one, Father, just as you are in me and I am in you." (John 17:21)

Jesus prayed for our unity.

Jesus prayed that our unity would be the same as the unity of the Trinity.

What is the response of the Father?

Think back to our simple parable. If the earthly father in that parable, being evil, would move heaven and earth to fulfill his daughter's last request … well, how much more will the heavenly Father, who holds all power and authority, work to fulfill his Son's last request?

As you read the story of Wittenberg 2017, you will see how the Father worked miracle after miracle. You will see the gentle progression of his will. You will see his patience as broken and fallible people stumble forward as best they can.

> Wittenberg 2017 is the story of a person. That Person is the heavenly Father.

You will see how he brought Roman Catholics, Protestants, Messianic Jews, and Eastern Orthodox together at the 500th anniversary of the Protestant Reformation, to grieve the divisions of the body of Christ, to celebrate the surprises of the Holy Spirit, and to pray with Jesus for the eventual full unity of the people of God.

I began by saying that Wittenberg 2017 is the story of a person. That Person is the heavenly Father. Wittenberg 2017 is a story of the Father's fierce resolve to answer his Son's prayer. It is only one of many such stories—past, present, and future. Maybe one of them will be yours.

Part I

Background and Vision,
1980s–2000

Chapter 1

Hope Chapel

This was surely one of the most memorable conferences we have ever attended, and we've been to many over the years. What we experienced was ecumenism in the deepest, truest sense of the word. There was heartfelt singing; moving mutual apologies made by Catholics and Lutherans to Anabaptists, and vice versa! There were hefty seminars on historical and theological topics that made us think, and opened our eyes; but also deeply stirring moments when people bared their souls. In between the larger gatherings, there were continual stimulating encounters with other seekers who were burning with the question of what it means to follow Christ. No one there was pushing an agenda, or "blowing their own horn," or engaging in identity politics. Instead, the conference was animated by a spirit of true togetherness, expectancy, and JOY.

CHRIS AND BEA ZIMMERMAN
Bruderhof (Anabaptist), England

The Lord brought Thomas and Amy into my life when they were in the high school youth group at Hope Chapel. They were part of the most extraordinary group of young people I have ever met. As they were married and through the years that followed, it was obvious to me that the Lord's hand of favor was upon them. When Thomas brought their vision for the Wittenberg meeting to me, it was totally consistent with the trajectory of how God had been leading them. But it was a big dream. Far bigger than anything that they could ever do without the Holy Spirit's prevenient grace at work in the hearts of the major church leaders in the many streams that make up his church.

DAN DAVIS, founding pastor of Hope Chapel
(Protestant / nondenominational), Austin, Texas USA

"This story needs to be written for the annals of reconciliation." These words surprised me with joy and wonder for they came from John Dawson, the leader of Youth With a Mission (YWAM) and one of my heroes in the faith. I never expected to have even a single conversation with this man. But in 2015 the Lord arranged our meeting on a prayer journey to Prague. During that trip I shared with him the vision of the Wittenberg 2017 initiative, which he ended up attending as one of the speakers. Some months after the event, he called and urged me to write this book.

As encouraging as John's words were, the astounding, humbling truth is that the Lord has already written this story—and all our stories—for his own remembrance. This is what the prophet Malachi says:

> Then those who feared the Lord talked with each other, and the Lord listened and heard. A scroll of remembrance was written in his presence concerning those who feared the Lord and honored His name. (Mal 3:16)

The implications are that God remembers …

> Every conversation that brings him glory.
> Every recounting of his goodness.
> Every discussion of his mercy.
> Every fearful phone call to an offended friend.
> All humble words of repentance, and each reply of forgiveness.

These are all recorded for eternity.

Certainly heaven was listening in the fall of 2017 when a remarkable group of people gathered in the medieval town of Wittenberg, Germany. They came in groups of twos, threes, and fours filing into the former seminary where Martin Luther taught in 1517, the year he formulated his Ninety-Five Theses. They traveled from many nations to observe the 500th anniversary of the Protestant Reformation. Nobody's attitude was triumphant celebration—not even the Lutherans. Instead, they gathered in grief over the hostile divisions in the body of Christ, desiring to pray John 17 with Jesus—"that they all will be one, Father, just as you are in me and I am in you." They came to sing, to teach, to reflect, to discuss, and to listen.

Who were these people filing through the doors?

They were Germans, Austrians, Swiss, Poles, Dutch, Britons, Norwegians, Hungarians, Slovaks, Serbs, Aussies, Kiwis, Israelis, Mexicans, Canadians, and Americans.

They were Roman Catholics, Lutherans, Presbyterians, Baptists, Anglicans, Pentecostals, nondenominational Evangelicals, Mennonites, Bruderhof, Amish, Eastern Orthodox, and Messianic Jews.

They were clergy and laity, missionaries, and nuns.

They were nobility and plain folk, scholars and students.

They were young and old, babies to octogenarians, men and women, boys and girls.

It was truly an amazing assembly—diverse, lively, august, wise.

The commissioning service at the very end of the 2017 gathering
was led by seven clergy and leaders from (left to right) the Pentecostal, Eastern Orthodox,
Anglican, Anabaptist, Lutheran, Roman Catholic, and Messianic Jewish traditions.
Photo by Ryan and Noleen Thurman. Used with permission.

And the people standing at the microphone to speak the words of welcome were ... my wife, Amy, and me.

How did we receive this honor?

How did a lay couple from Texas find themselves welcoming priests and pastors to a quintessentially German event?

That is one of the many "surprises of the Holy Spirit" in this story—the story of Wittenberg 2017.[1]

Telling the story requires going back in time. Back to the year 1980. Back to a sequence of events that while perhaps quiet and seemingly commonplace were nonetheless significant. When Amy, my future wife, was in middle

---

1   My original title for the book was "Surprises of the Spirit," which was a frequent saying of Father Peter Hocken's—and how he characterized the Wittenberg 2017 initiative.

school, her family faced a decision. They were planning to move from their home in New Mexico either to Colorado Springs or back to their native state of Texas. Colorado Springs was an attractive choice considering the fact that they were living at the time in a ski village with breathtaking views. It is hard to leave the beauty of the mountains.

Her family took an exploratory trip to Colorado, looking for homes and job opportunities. Just as they arrived, an out-of-season snowstorm struck. Would I have met Amy otherwise? Only God knows, of course, but I like to think that he sent that freak snowstorm in 1980. As her whole family sat shivering in Colorado Springs, the heat of central Texas began to sound pretty good!

The Craver family moved to Austin, the city where I was born and raised. In the mid-1970s, my parents were moving on from a Jesus People church called The Well. It had been a wonderful environment for a young child. I had surrendered my life to Jesus and was baptized there at the age of seven. However, The Well dissolved as the leadership team fell apart. My family joined a group that moved on to St. David's Episcopal, a historic downtown church.

Soon I was in junior high, with all that that implies. Puberty, hormones, temptations, and peer pressure were in full swing. During services at St. David's, I sat bored in the pews until I could manufacture an acceptable reason to leave the service, wander through the building or surrounding streets, and uncover any mischief I could find.

My parents, somewhat in desperation, lured me to a Christian summer camp by telling me it was a sports camp. Indeed, we did play basketball and tennis during the day, but at night we sang songs, prayed, and listened to evangelistic messages from the camp counselors. I remember one night vividly. I wandered out to the soccer goal, looked up at the stars, and told Jesus that I wanted to live only for him. So at age seven I had been saved by Jesus; but at age fourteen I became a disciple of Jesus.

Shortly after I got back to Austin, my best friend called. "Thomas, I found an awesome youth group—do you want to come next week?" Of course I did! And I loved it. After that first Wednesday night youth meeting, I told my parents, "You can stay at St. David's, but I am going to Hope Chapel!"[2]

---

2 My parents graciously followed me and became integrated into the local church life of Hope Chapel.

Hope Chapel is where I met Amy. It is also where I formed other lifelong friendships that would play a role in the Wittenberg 2017 story. When I look back at that decision, and all that has come from it, I am in awe—and a little frightened. God entrusted an immature young teenager with a life-altering decision. I don't know that I would have done that. God's tolerance for risk seems to me much higher than ours.

This aspect of God's character—tolerance for risk—was well represented at Hope Chapel, a small independent, nondenominational church. It was founded in 1977 by Dan Davis.

Dan Davis with his wife, Joann, in the early days of Hope Chapel. Photo courtesy of Dan and Joann Davis. Used with permission.

Dan had left his position as a marketing executive at Intel to start the church. Being trained in business rather than at seminary, Dan held some leadership values uncharacteristic of typical church administration. One of those values was the celebration of failure. If someone in the church tried something new, and failed, he would throw a party to celebrate! This encouraged everyone in the pews to take risks. As a result, Hope Chapel became a church where new initiatives were continually started, with the full support of church leadership.

Another of Dan's gifts was his vision for church unity. Dan saw that many senior pastors suffered from loneliness as a result of competitiveness. He also saw the damage this competition did to the kingdom of God in a city. Dan countered this division by continually teaching his flock, "There is only one church in the city! It meets in many places, but it is only one church." As his influence grew among other pastors in Austin, this idea began to take hold. Today Austin is blessed with remarkable unity among the Protestant pastors, and Dan is largely credited with leading the way in forming relationships, fostering cooperation, and encouraging honor among the city's pastors.

I grew up sitting under Dan's preaching, and these twin ideas of risk and unity became part of my normal Christian life. The Hope Chapel youth group, led by Jayson Knox, mirrored these values as well. We kids were always proposing crazy ventures, and Jayson's answer was invariably "Sure, let's try it!" Jayson formed relationships with other youth leaders around the city, and we would go on retreats together or interact in other ways. One of his friends happened to be the youth leader at St. Ignatius Catholic Church in South Austin—and I remember visiting their youth group, blissfully unaware of what Catholic even meant!

I also remember the day that Amy Craver walked into one of our youth group meetings. My immediate attraction to this intelligent blonde girl who loved the Lord was foiled by the steady stream of boyfriends that she had. By the time I found out she had broken up with one, she was already going steady with another! Oh well … he who laughs last, laughs best.

Amy and I were married at Hope Chapel on July 21, 1990. We planned to become overseas missionaries. In 1986, we had together taken one of the first offerings of the now-legendary course *Perspectives on the World Christian Movement*. Hope Chapel was sending teams into the 10/40 Window. Amy pursued a college degree in linguistics, and I obtained a business degree, both with the same goal—fruitfulness on the mission field. In the late 1990s, we moved with our two young children into a mostly Hispanic neighborhood in East Austin, with the goal of living cross-culturally until we could go overseas to the Middle East.

And then God sprang on our happy little family a series of surprises. The path he laid before us led instead to Wittenberg, Germany—and to the year 2017.

Use the QR code or visit **https://bit.ly/w17ch01** to explore more pictures and additional material for this chapter, including the reason why nobody saw our wedding kiss.

Chapter 2

Born Again, Again

Even everything that has been playing out in our own family these last few weeks was not conceivable before. Our children, who live very far away from each other, meet with us and the grandchildren every evening at 7:30 for a devotional, to pray together and sing, and the next generation is doing this. Many young people are coming to us with questions. In our church, young people invited my generation, the grandparent generation, to a weekend of fellowship, and they invited three old women because being intergenerational has become important to them. There is a great blessing on this.

CHRISTINE HEROLD, Evangelical Lutheran Church,
Neudrossenfeld, Germany, also member of the Kreuzbruderschaft
(Fellowship of the Cross), Ottmaring, Germany

I was radically impacted by the John 17 focus and the prophetic image of the empty seat at the table to make the circle of four.[1] This was a clear confirmation for me, and the Lord warmed me with his love over and over through the worship and ministry of the sessions. You see, I had experienced in August 2017 three weeks of high blood pressure, over 200, with no response from medicine. In the midst of this issue, Jesus met me in a dream and spoke John 17:22–23 over me as an invitation to become one with them—the Father, Son, and Holy Spirit. It was so real I felt his presence, and as I moved toward him immediately the high blood pressure broke and has not been high since.

LLOYD HOOVER, bishop, Lancaster Mennonite Conference
(Anabaptist), Lancaster, Pennsylvania USA

---

1 This refers to a large original triptych painting by John Michael Wall that was on stage during the final 2017 gathering in Wittenberg. The painting is a modern interpretation of Rublev's well-known icon of Abraham's Three Visitors. Franziskus Eisenbach explained in a talk at the Trento gathering (2014) that Rublev's symbolism is of the Trinity, and that there is a "seat at the table" for mankind—an invitation to enter into the unity of the Trinity. In this way, Rublev's icon and thus John Michael's painting both visually depict Jesus's prayer for us, found in John 17:21–26. Use the QR code at the end of the chapter to view both the icon and the painting.

The year must have been 1998 when Amy and I were facing the difficult decision of leaving Mission Hills Church.[2] I say this because I know that our daughter Peggy Jo was three years old. She was at that cute age where she would sit down with a pad of paper and a crayon and draw a big scribble. Amy would ask, "What's that, Peggy?"

"A horsey!" Peggy would proudly reply.

Of course, before Amy could say, "That's a really good horse," Peggy's big brother Noah, all of six years old, would scornfully interject, "That doesn't look anything like a horse." Peggy filled her lungs and let loose the sibling scream, "Nooo-AHH!!" He giggled and ran, and so went the next hour ...

Noah and Peggy with Amy (1997).
Photo by Thomas Cogdell.

One particular Saturday morning, I had just awakened from a vivid dream.

I was packing a pickup truck in front of our house. Amy came out the front door. "Amy," I told her, "it's time to get in the truck, and go. Tell the children." She quickly reappeared with Noah and Peggy Jo. We all climbed into the truck and drove away.

When I awoke from the dream around 6:00 AM, Amy was already stirring, so I recounted the dream to her. "Amy," I said, "I think God may be telling us it's OK to leave the church." She sleepily agreed and I headed off to the restroom.

To get to the bathroom in this house, I had to walk through Peggy's room. Peggy Jo was not a child you wanted to wake once she had achieved the rare, blessed state called "sleep" ... so I entered quietly. To my surprise,

---

2 Mission Hills Church was a daughter church plant from Hope Chapel. Jayson Knox, our youth pastor at Hope, had helped to lead this church plant the year we graduated from high school, so it was natural to follow along in his footsteps. Jayson later resigned as senior pastor and moved to Phoenix to join the staff of Antioch Network (a missions-oriented ministry founded by George Miley and Dan Davis, which will play a large role later in the book). After Jayson's departure, Mission Hills had a season of searching to find its identity, and it was in this season that Amy and I were struggling with whether or not it would be best for the church if we left.

Peggy was already up, sitting at her desk, coloring a big scribble. I blurted out the first thing that came into my mind, "Peggy, what are you coloring?"

My little girl looked up at me and said, "I'm coloring Daddy saying it's time to get in the truck and go."

My jaw hit the floor!

What do you do with that? I mean, telling someone else their dream is exactly what all the wise men of Nebuchadnezzar's court *couldn't* do. The fact that Daniel could tell the king his dream astonished everyone. And I was astonished at Peggy's matter-of-fact words. But also exhilarated— God was speaking at six in the morning! I went back immediately and told Amy, "Honey, I think God just confirmed that interpretation of the dream!"

This dream came in a season of great change in our lives. While many of our life circumstances were challenging, we were in the midst of a glorious season of spiritual awakening—a time that Amy and I speak about as "being born again, *again!*" Though we had always believed in the Holy Spirit and had some experience with the Spirit's power, we were discovering the Holy Spirit's intimate knowledge of us. We were learning how to hear his voice and trust him. God was constantly breaking into our everyday existence and wowing us with his Reality. We were learning that God was truly Real.

> And our hearts were pounding in those days–Oh, were they pounding!

Of course, if you had given us a true/false quiz before this season, we would have correctly chosen: "God is real—True." But it's one thing to know it in your mind, and quite another to have that knowledge penetrate the very core of your being. "Surely you desire truth in the inner parts; you teach me wisdom in the inmost place," writes the psalmist. The Father was inscribing his love on our hearts through the Holy Spirit. And our hearts were pounding in those days—Oh, were they pounding! Each morning Amy and I would wake up, look at each other, and ask, "What is God going to do today?"

During that season we had frequent, vivid dreams. The Lord was instructing our hearts in the night, as David writes in the Psalms. We also began to receive prophetic words—a new experience for us. Scriptures we had read a hundred times suddenly came to life. Most importantly, we fell in love with worship and prayer. We couldn't get enough of it.

Like young lovers lost in each other, we were also pretty foolish at times. We had never experienced a season like this before. We couldn't wait to tell everyone we knew about the latest wild vision, or the dynamic preacher we had just discovered, or the new album that immediately ranked among the best in the history of Christendom. When they didn't seem to relate, we were honestly surprised.

In our immaturity, we made several mistakes. If we were to relive those days now, we would surely speak with more discernment. But in retrospect, we see the mistakes as part of the plan. What was happening in this season? God was revealing that he could speak to us—in our own language. We were in the "voice of God" school. Learning what was *not* from God was as valuable as learning what *was* from God. And when a word or impression was from God, learning how *not* to respond was as important as learning how *to* respond.

These lessons were foundational for the paths God would call us to walk that led to Wittenberg 2017.

There was one particular dream that God gave to Amy in those days that proved significant for that journey. To understand it, some background information is necessary.

The Denver City Church of Christ.
Photo by Thomas Cogdell.

Amy grew up in Denver City—a small oilfield town in far West Texas that didn't really need to add "City" to avoid being confused with the capital of Colorado. All of Amy's family attended the Denver City Church of Christ, a conservative Protestant denomination. No musical instruments were used in church services. Women were not allowed in leadership positions, and all the male leaders sat together in the front of the church.

At the time Amy had the dream, she was the leader of an inner-city ministry in Austin called City Girls for Jesus. The City Girls were a group of young women between the ages of nine and fifteen who met once a week in our home for crafts, fun, and Bible study. The ministry was somewhere between a church youth group and a girl scout troop. Many of the girls came from Mexican-American Catholic families.

In the dream, Amy was walking with the City Girls into the door of the Church of Christ in Denver City.

"This is not going to go well," she anticipated, remembering the anti-Hispanic and anti-Catholic attitudes of her childhood church.

The first thing that happened in the dream was that two women came out with guitars and sang a beautiful version of "Humble Thyself in the Sight of the Lord."

Amy was, of course, quite surprised.

Then the preacher stood up from his seat in the midst of the congregation (not from the front where he normally would sit) and announced, "I'm not going to preach today. Instead, I have invited a young, Catholic, Hispanic woman named Nina to give the sermon."

Young? Hispanic? Catholic? Woman? That was four strikes, not just three! But Amy was very relieved in the dream, thinking that her City Girls would at least not be offended by the sermon.

Nina came to the pulpit and began to speak about the saints, and Amy found the sermon very beautiful.

Amy understood that the dream was about unity in the Church. She knew this was Jesus's desire for his Church … but she didn't know what it had to do with her.

Later on in this story, you will see that Amy actually meets Nina. Yes, she was a real person! That's what life was like, in the season of being "born again, again." The Holy Spirit was directing our thoughts and our paths, and it was wonderful!

Use the QR code or visit **https://bit.ly/w17ch02** to explore more pictures and additional material for this chapter, including another important dream that God gave to Amy during this season of our life.

Chapter 3

Power Plant of Prayer

We were so struck by the power of reconciliation at the Wittenberg 2017 gathering—most especially the power of prayer, repentance, and forgiveness. We also wanted to put something into practice when we returned, so in January 2018 we began hosting monthly dinners in our home to bring together Christians in our city (Worcester, MA) from various church traditions to share our stories and grow in love for one another. This has opened many doors of friendship and reconciliation in our city through folk who were part of these dinners.

SCOTT AND CLAIRE BRILL, Lutheran and Evangelical,
Assistant Regional Director for InterVarsity New England;
Founding Fellow and co-director at Institute for Christian Unity;
Leadership Council Chair, The Initiative, Worcester, Massachusetts USA

Our involvement included leading three night-watch sessions. We were able to rise and get to the prayer chapel, a cozy basement room with a window and a large cross on the wall, by 4:20 AM to get settled for our prayer time. Each morning began with thirty minutes of Bridge Prayer that we shared with the previous team (hence the name, Bridge Prayer), followed by leading prayer and worship for a surprisingly full room of eager worshippers until 7:30. We would then walk and pray back to the main location for the daytime sessions (4:30 to 8:00 AM total).

Perhaps others were jet-lagged and naturally rose around 4:00 AM, or perhaps it was just hunger and excitement at what God was doing in and through this gathering, but we had several participants each morning including pastors and laypeople as well as more than one member of the German nobility who were involved in Wittenberg 2017. It is perhaps a point not to be made too much of, but I personally felt honored that they saw it worthwhile to come, to stay (the whole 2.5–3 hours), and come back again.

MICHAEL AND JOELENE MICHEL, Hope Chapel,
Christ the Reconciler Community, Austin, Texas USA

During this season of frequent encounters with God, Amy and I grew much closer to our friends Phillip and Caroline Owens. Phillip had been a high school freshman in the Hope Chapel youth group when I showed up there in 1983, so Amy and I had known him for over a decade. He was a talented musician and ended up as the drummer for One Bad Pig, the first Christian punk band to break through into the mainstream. Decades later, Phillip would be the primary worship leader for Wittenberg 2017!

Phillip and Caroline were having similar experiences to ours—dreams and visions, growth in love for prayer and worship, and strange looks from other people. We began to search together for help to grow in our ability to respond more maturely.

And we found that help in Metro Christian Fellowship in Kansas City. The history of MCF includes a number of dramatic prophetic encounters, seasons of controversy and criticism, and a growing emphasis on worship and prayer. We were excited to find a community that thought it normal for God to speak in surprising ways. The four of us began to drive up to Kansas City every few months to attend MCF conferences.

There were a number of good teachers at MCF, but I found myself responding particularly to Mike Bickle, the senior pastor. Mike had developed a lengthy teaching series on the Song of Songs—an unlikely book of the Bible for a man who looked and spoke like a football coach.[1]

In particular, one phrase captivated me: "I am dark, but lovely," the bride says in Song of Songs 1:5 (NKJV). Understanding myself as part of the Bride of Christ, my heart began to sing this song—"I am sinful, but still beautiful to God." I had always unconsciously assumed that one day, when I got my act together, God would then like me. Sure, God *loved* me now—in the sense that he self-sacrificially tolerated me. But it never occurred to me that God might actually *like* me now. That he might find me beautiful, even while I saw only warts, weakness, and immaturity.

"I am dark, but lovely" … Wow! This understanding liberated my heart from sinful patterns of thought. I would now just stand in the middle of the sidewalk, grinning up at God—"You like me! You really do!" All of my previous habits of prayer melted away like an old dirty snowbank on the

---

1 To this day, whenever I see Bill Belichick on the sidelines of an NFL game, I think: "Mike Bickle."

first glorious day of spring. Prayer had before been a burdensome mix of duty and performance. Now it was truly enjoyable—to just stand in the presence of the Lover of my soul, gazing upward with a goofy smile on my face.[2]

On February 14, 1999, I was walking early in the morning on a trail near our house. It was still dark. Looming overhead was the Holly Street Power Plant, a constant source of light and noise in the primarily Spanish-speaking neighborhood where we lived. I was always fascinated by this structure of steel pipes with the steam rising, and the wires radiating outward into various parts of the city. As I stood looking at it, suddenly a phrase popped into my mind.

"Power plant of prayer."

Where did that come from? What did that even mean? Our recent years of training in discerning the voice of God proved very helpful at this point— I knew it was the Lord speaking, not my own imagination.

But … what did that mean?

> I wondered–is there power missing for the churches in the city, because there's not a power plant of prayer?

I thought about the fact that electricity cannot be easily stored. For example, a city can store up water for its citizens in a reservoir. If there is a drought, the extra water is important. But there is no way to make a lake of electricity! Electricity must be consumed at just the moment when it is generated. For example, when Peggy cried in the middle of the night and I switched on the light in her room, someone somewhere was manning a power plant that was generating the electricity that coursed at that millisecond through the filament of the light bulb, chasing away the scary shadows for my daughter.

I wondered—is there power missing for the churches in the city, because there's not a power plant of prayer? Is someone crying out for deliverance in the middle of the night, but there's "no electricity" because nobody is manning the power plant of prayer? It was not an attempt to form a new theology—just a thought, just a wondering. I wrote it in my journal, and even drew a picture of the "power plant of prayer" … then promptly

---

2 My family and friends call this my "Snoopy pose," after the funny dance of the famous beagle in Charles Shulz's cartoon strip.

forgot about it! (I get lots of crazy ideas, and most of them leave as easily as they come.)

Well, just a few months later I traveled to Kansas City for a conference. On May 7, 1999, I was sitting on the risers in the back of MCF when Mike Bickle unexpectedly announced:

> *Tonight we're going to interrupt the main conference to do something special. We are launching a 24-7 house of prayer, starting tonight. Let's pray for the first team, and give them the key to go unlock the prayer room and start up day and night prayer.*

Immediately the image of the power plant of prayer came back. This was that!

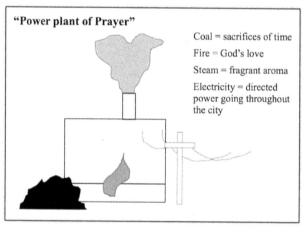

The picture I drew in my (electronic) journal on February 14, 1999.

I traveled back to Austin, convinced that God was calling me to start a house of prayer. My mind was full of plans, people to connect with, vision to communicate.

For some reason ... I never mentioned this to Amy.

Use the QR code or visit **https://bit.ly/w17ch03** to explore more pictures and additional material for this chapter, including a picture of Johnny Cash shooting Silly String at Phillip Owens.

Chapter 4

God's Landmine

By Amy Cogdell

On the journey to Wittenberg, God graciously used brothers and sisters from different church backgrounds to bring to light the ignorance and arrogance in our hearts. We learned much about practicing reconciliation in everyday life. We can never forget the times of repentance for the sins of our denominations in the Volkenroda chapel and later in St. Peter's Basilica in Rome. Thank you, Thomas and Amy, for your obedience to the Lord and your wise leadership in the face of many challenges.

DAVID AND GREETJE SANDERS,
Protestant / nondenominational, Berlin, Germany

For me, there were two worship services we celebrated together that were of unforgettable significance. One of these was a Sunday service in Rome in the small church in the Catacombs. It was not a Eucharistic worship service. All of the pastors present, working in pairs, washed the feet of those attending the service. Then the Sunday readings were presented. Instead of the usual presentation of the gifts of the altar, we offered ourselves and our world to God as a gift to transform. Then we did the passing of the peace and sending to be witnesses.

The other worship service I cannot forget is the final one we celebrated in the large conference hall in Wittenberg. The pastors of all the churches represented and all confessions (Messianic Jews, Catholics, Orthodox Christians, Evangelical Christians, Anglicans, Pentecostals, Baptists) were sitting in a large semicircle on the stage. One after the other, they confessed the guilt of their respective faith communities with respect to the lost unity of Christendom, asked God and their siblings in Christ for forgiveness, and pledged to be witnesses for and to serve in Christian unity.

Both of these worship services were an image of the longed-for unity among us and a powerful plea to God to send us this unity again in answer to Jesus's own prayer.

FRANZISKUS EISENBACH, Roman Catholic, auxiliary bishop
emeritus of Mainz, Germany

*I asked Amy to write this chapter. After all, it's her story ... —*Thomas Cogdell

When one becomes accustomed to hearing the voice of God, his silence is terrible. I don't mean the kind of silence that is the absence of words. Quietness, even dryness, is a necessary part of our spiritual walk. But there is a type of silence in which God withholds himself because his word is not received, and that is unbearable.

Amy's friend Margaret shortly after her conversion, on a camping trip in Big Bend National Park. Photo by Thomas Cogdell.

I (Amy) had provoked the Lord's silence with my resistance. He had spoken quite plainly, but I was afraid of his instruction. My assignment was simple. He wanted me to call my high school friend Margaret and deliver a message on his behalf.[1] "Tell her that I say she is an excellent mother." There was nothing fearful in those words, only blessing. Even so, I was unwilling.

"Lord," I replied, "What if Margaret thinks I am crazy or presumptuous? That would make it harder for us to speak about you."

Margaret was, perhaps, the smartest person I had ever known. She excelled at math, writing, foreign language, everything academic. We were roommates for a few months our freshman year of college. I recall several mornings, sitting at the table with the newspaper laid out before me, when Margaret would walk up behind me and begin to read over my shoulder. While I was still halfway through the first article, she would gently pull up the corner of the front page to read the page underneath, and then the next. Her mind was not only faster than mine, but broader as well. Margaret thought about issues that I had never considered. My first lessons in politics, fair trade, and social justice all came from Margaret. I admired her greatly, but I was a bit intimidated by her intellect.

During our first year at university, Margaret experienced a dramatic conversion. Faith seemed to overtake her suddenly as a powerful wave,

---

1 Not her real name.

effecting a beautiful transformation in its wake. Her speech, which could cut opponents to pieces, softened with charity. Her innate sense of justice turned to service. Even her physical appearance changed.

Margaret came to faith in the Catholic Church, which was entirely unfamiliar to me. To say my family mistrusted Catholicism would be an understatement. I heard as a child that Catholics were idolaters. They believed strange doctrines. They prayed to dead people and worshipped Mary. Honestly, I found all of this hard to believe. No intelligent person would really worship idols, I thought. All the same, I was wary of Catholics and decidedly uncomfortable around icons, incense, and liturgy.

The first Catholic Mass I attended was Easter vigil for Margaret's confirmation. All I remember clearly was the fire lit outside on the sidewalk by the University Catholic Center. The church itself was dark and empty. Those gathered outside were similarly silent and solemn. The priest lit a large Easter candle from the fire outside, and without a word we followed him into the church. Later, one candle was lit from the Christ candle. The fire was passed up and down the rows, lighting individual handheld candles. I was impressed by what a beautiful, fitting image this was for my friend—Margaret was now carrying the light of Christ.

I learned a few things about the Catholic faith that year, mostly as Margaret asked me questions about what I believed. I enjoyed our conversations, but I did not delve deeply into the peculiarities of Catholic doctrine. It was clear to me that God was at work in Margaret. I knew she was keenly intelligent. As she studied scripture, I assumed she would see the errors of Catholic practice and settle into a faith more like my own. That never happened.

Margaret and I both moved away after college. We married and had children. We saw each other once or twice each year when we were home for the holidays. Group gatherings were seldom conducive to theological exploration, and years passed in which we had no significant spiritual dialogue. So it seemed abrupt to call her on the phone and deliver a "word from God." I told the Lord I did not think Catholics were into that sort of thing.

He was not impressed.

For several minutes I sat in the silence of his displeasure. Slowly it dawned on me that I would not hear him speak again until I obeyed. This was a mercy rather than a punishment. One who is untrustworthy with little should not be given more. I desperately wanted to hear God again, so I picked up the phone with a trembling hand.

My window of opportunity would be short. I had two preschoolers who were occupied at the moment. Margaret had a toddler. Chances that we were both free seemed slim. I hoped she would be too busy to pick up the phone. Leaving a message would be easier than waiting for her response. But of course, the Lord was well aware of the timing.

> "Amy," Margaret confided, "I have also been having dreams—dreams about you."

Margaret answered the phone. I dutifully delivered my message and tried to end the call quickly. Margaret, however, was not so eager to hang up. She was hungry, it seemed, for deep conversation. We talked for over an hour, and as we spoke, I realized that I was also hungry. For months my heart had been burning with a newfound love for God, but few were open to hearing, except for Thomas and our friends Phillip and Caroline Owens. Margaret was different. I felt a freedom with her I did not expect. I found myself telling her about the dreams I had been having—especially the one set in my grandparents' church where Catholics and Protestants worshipped together. Then the tables turned.

"Amy," Margaret confided, "I have also been having dreams—dreams about you—dreams in which you and I share the Eucharist. And Amy," she continued, "I've been aching to ask you all these years, why aren't you Catholic?"

I was shocked into silence. Margaret wanted me to be Catholic? But I was the older sister in the faith! I had prayed for Margaret years before she believed in Christ. I grew up steeped in scripture. I was filled with the Holy Spirit. And still Margaret saw something lacking in my faith. How could that be?

I felt as if I had stepped on a landmine. Something exploded in my soul. I was disoriented. Afraid. Frozen.

My first instinct was to close the wound. Shut the door. I was touched that Margaret had been so vulnerable with me. In truth, I had never loved her so much as I did in that moment. But what she imagined could never be! I had to make that clear. It would be wrong for me to foster any false hope. Wrong to entertain such a thought!

Fumbling for words, I tried to affirm our unity in Christ, but I told Margaret bluntly that I could never be Catholic. I simply did not believe the teachings of the Catholic Church. She apologized for overstepping, and our phone call ended abruptly.

My heart ached. Not only was I reeling from some invisible wound, I had hurt my friend. The rejection I had feared from her was precisely what I offered in response to her gift of revelation. But what else could I have said in truth?

On some level I felt betrayed. It was clear that the Lord had initiated this call more for my sake than for Margaret's, yet I could make no sense of its ending. My head was spinning. I could not pray.

Nighttime brought the relief of quiet. With Thomas and the kids in bed, I tried to process what had transpired that afternoon. I read the promise from Ezekiel that the houses of Israel and Judah would be reunited into one "stick" in the Lord's hand. I prayed for this miracle to extend to the Church, to Catholics and Protestants as well. I wrote a long letter to Margaret, but still I felt no peace.

At 2:00 AM I was still awake, pacing around our dining room table. Suddenly a sharp, physical pain hit my heart. I fell to the floor clutching my chest. I understood immediately that I was experiencing the pain that Jesus feels over the divisions in his Body. This pain was like the pain of a divorce spanning centuries, sickening billions of souls. It was a pain only Christ could bear. The head of the Church suffers when his members are at war with one another, separated by historical injury, by ignorance, contempt, and pride. If this pain had lasted more than a few seconds, I believe it would have killed me. But for just a moment, our Savior allowed me to share his grief. Panting on the ground, I found myself saying over and over again, "Thank you, Jesus! Thank you, Jesus!" He had given me a gift of intimacy beyond all I had ever known.

Use the QR code or visit **https://bit.ly/w17ch04** to explore more pictures and additional material for this chapter, including a funny story of how Peggy convinced us to baptize her at age six.

Chapter 5

Switzerland

A blessed and memorable experience. I loved the sharing that took place, with various religious lenses. Christ was present and we received signs. I remember the thunder during one of our gatherings. The Father, the Son, and Holy Spirit spoke to us in so many ways. Our hearts were opened. I was privileged to meet so many of God's people, outside my bubble. Thank you, Amy and Thomas, for the invitation, and your welcoming!

FLORA RUIZ, Roman Catholic, Archdiocese Pastoral Council,
Los Angeles, California USA

It was a great joy to attend a preparatory meeting for Wittenberg 2017, and to share fascinating historical parallels between the Protestant Reformation and the nation of Israel.

It begins in 1492 when the Jews experienced the traumatic Spanish expulsion, which forced them to either convert to Catholicism or leave. Unexpectedly the leader of the Ottoman Empire, Suleiman the Magnificent, sent ships to carry Spanish Jews to his lands. Twenty-five years later, two monumental events occurred simultaneously: in 1517, Suleiman would be favored to conquer Jerusalem, allowing the first Jews to return; and in 1517, Martin Luther would publish his Ninety-Five Theses to the church! As Luther's favor and prominence grew in the decades to follow, so, too, would Suleiman's. He would not only gain lands; he would fully rebuild the walls of Jerusalem as they stand today! The Ottomans would rule the Holy Land for exactly 400 years, until the British, under a devout Christian, General Allenby, would score a daring and decisive victory at the key city of Beersheba. That very day, with the signers knowing nothing about that victory, the famous Balfour Declaration was signed in London. The date? You guessed it! October 31, 1917—400 years to the day from when Luther published his theses! So simultaneously as the 500th anniversary was being celebrated in Wittenberg, Israel and Great Britain were celebrating the 100th anniversary of events that helped Israel to become a nation! God is amazing!

ROBERT O'DELL, Hope Chapel (Protestant / nondenominational),
co-founder of Root Source, Austin, Texas USA

Many of my most inspired ideas have come to me in the bathtub. So I continually raise the odds by taking ever longer baths. Sometimes more than once a day.

One of my favorite bathtubs was the upstairs tub in my parents' historic house in Austin, where I grew up. A green tub, with colorful tiles all around on the floor. There were three identical knobs—one for hot, one for cold (which I hardly touched), and one for letting the water drain—when you turned it to this position, it ominously read "Waste," as if it were a century-old prophet of modern-day water issues. It was in this green upstairs bathtub that I had the brilliant idea to pursue Amy Craver until she married me.

My father had strictly forbidden reading in the tub—I guess for fear that I would ruin the book by dropping it into the water. My youthful workaround to this conundrum was to hide the contraband book in a towel. When I became the master of my own destiny, I had the freedom to create a bathtub space with not only a reading light, but also a skylight! I designed this bathing architectural wonder when we remodeled an old house on Canterbury Street in Austin in 1998. With its clear glass skylight spanning the length of the tub, it was a good thing that drones were not omnipresent back then.

I had also always wanted, but never had, a clawfoot tub. So I amused my wife by taking her to antique stores in small Texas towns, where I proceeded to lie down in each dusty bathtub to make sure it was comfortable enough for me.[1]

It was from that Canterbury clawfoot tub that I announced to Amy, "I'm taking you to Switzerland!" Her response told me the bathtub muse was at work again: "How did you know that I have always wanted to go to Switzerland?!"

The occasion was our tenth wedding anniversary.

The problem was that we didn't have enough money to go to Switzerland.

But when Amy gets excited about something, she begins to research. And that night, she got on the computer and began to look at the various prices and itineraries to Europe. A few nights later, on a Thursday evening,

---

1 The Dante in me believes there will be a special level in hell where the designers of hotel bathtubs have to lie for eternity in their neck-cricking creations.

she told me that she had found the cheapest prices yet—not that we could afford them, but they were better than all the others. "Should I put them on our credit card?"

We decided to put them on a twenty-four-hour hold, sleep on it, and decide in the morning.

That night I had a dream.

> *I was with Amy in front of a store—like a classic fifties department store, with the most desirable items displayed in the window. Amy really, really wanted what was in that window (what it was, I couldn't quite make out in the dream). I was very sad because I didn't have enough money to buy it for her. We turned away. As I was getting into the car to drive off, I glanced down. There, in the gutter, were three gold coins. Curious, I picked them up. Each of them had the number 1,000 on them, and also my name! "I guess these belong to me," I thought in the dream. And I was suddenly very happy, because now I could buy Amy whatever was in that window.*

When I woke up Friday morning, I told Amy the dream. "I think this means we should buy the tickets," I said. So Amy made the purchase.

The next week, I was at my work office and the phone rang. "Thomas, you won't believe what happened!!" It was Amy. "I just got our bank statement in the mail, and on Friday morning, $3,000 appeared in our bank account!" I was amazed. God had done it again!

Amy had no idea where the money came from, because at that time direct deposit was not a normal way to exchange money. Much later, we got a notice from the IRS that they had recalculated our taxes for us and decided that they owed us $3,000 back—which they direct-deposited in the same account they had so freely withdrawn from. Would it

We made it to Switzerland and snapped this tenth-anniversary photo beneath the Matterhorn. Photo by Thomas Cogdell.

have been more of a miracle for the money to just have appeared ... or for the IRS to have voluntarily sent it to us? You decide ...

I find this entire episode to be so wonderfully revealing of the glorious mystery of God's ways. When we made the decision to purchase the tickets on Friday morning, the money was already in our bank account. But we didn't know it, and so we acted on faith to make the purchase. Did God sovereignly act? Yes. But he also graciously gave us the dignity of a faith-filled choice. Oh, the beauty of the mystery of the interweaving of his sovereignty with our ability to choose freely! All praise and glory to him!

So in late May, when we drove to the airport, we had great confidence that this trip was ordained by God. We had just left our children—Noah, Peggy, and our new little one-year-old, Justus—with Phillip and Caroline and their three children, who were about the same ages.

On the plane, our conversation was all about one topic—should Amy become Catholic?

Why was this? To explain requires going back in time a little.

After her experience of the grief of God on the day she talked to Margaret, Amy had decided she should visit the local Catholic church. It was the center of life in our Hispanic neighborhood, and it was just down the road—but we had never gone inside.

Amy set up an appointment with the priest, Father Larry Mattingly. Nervous, she stammered about wanting to serve in some way, such as driving people to church, or mopping the floors. Father Larry wisely asked a few questions and learned about Amy's experience mentoring teenage girls. "Why don't you help out with the youth group? You can see Sister Guadalupe Medina on Tuesday."

Sister Guadalupe Medina? Amy had never met a nun before. She waited with trepidation outside the office, until a short, smiling woman in a habit emerged. Amy didn't get any further than "Sister Guadalupe, I ..." before she was grabbed by the arm and guided down the hallway. "Father Larry told me you'd be coming, Amy," Sister Guadalupe said as she opened the door to a room, and then announced to the dozen Hispanic teenagers:

"This is Amy, your new youth leader." Amy was shocked. She leaned over and whispered to Sister Guadalupe, "But I'm not Catholic," to which the nun replied, "Oh, that doesn't matter, let's start planning tonight's youth meeting." Amy was in a daze as the group of young adults, who represented the youth leadership core, gathered together.

"Let's start with games." (*"I understand that,"* Amy thought, *"Protestants have games too."*)

"Next we'll have the talk." (*"OK, this is not too weird yet …"*)

"Then we'll have the altar call." (*"Wait … the altar call?!?"*)

This time Amy spoke out her thoughts. "Um … what do you mean by … 'altar call'?"

They looked at her. "It's when we invite people up to the front to receive Jesus," they said—with the implied message: "Don't you know anything?"

Well, just like that Amy's preconceptions about Catholics began to be washed away in the joy and life of the youth group at Cristo Rey Catholic Church in East Austin. She fell in love with them, and they fell in love with her. And one of the leaders in that core group was … wait for it … Nina! Yes, at Cristo Rey Amy actually met the girl she had seen years earlier in her City Girls dream.

In one youth meeting, the topic of Protestant evangelists came up. When leaving Mass, the students would be sometimes be met by people encouraging them to leave the Catholic Church, accept Jesus, and come to their church. This puzzled some of the young people. So they asked Amy, "You're Protestant, do you know why they do this?"

Put on the spot, Amy nervously replied, "Well, they do it because they believe that idol worship is against God's laws; and that when you pray to Mary, you are worshipping idols; so they don't want you to go to hell." To her surprise, the students began applauding. They were relieved that these evangelists were sincere in wanting them to know God better, and just misunderstood their faith practices. Amy learned a lot that day.

Amy had also been invited by Margaret to join an online email group discussing matters of Catholic theology and practice. Amy didn't type and didn't have email—but more worrying to her was having to set these Catholics straight about their theological errors. She quickly discovered that the group had very good answers to her questions and objections. As she told me later, "Catholics have had a long time to think about these things." Bible verses that seemed to her to obviously have one meaning were explained from a Catholic point of view, which was like viewing the same mountain from different vantage points. Amy realized not that the Catholic interpretation was always right, but that it was usually reasonable.

One of her biggest concerns was the hierarchical structure of the Roman Catholic Church. In our nondenominational experiences, we had absorbed a certain interpretation of Acts 2:42 as God's ideal: small, informal, unstructured meetings in the believers' houses. Big churches equaled man-made religion. Liturgical worship that was not spontaneous could not be Spirit-led.

Amy decided to find out for herself. She bought a series on the early church fathers, from before AD 100 through about AD 600. Her journey through their writings taught her that from the first generation of Christians onward, a highly organized church existed with liturgical elements that were not at all informal or unstructured.

She also began going to Mass. This was not in place of attending Hope Chapel, but at other times. Amy would leave in the early morning for liturgical prayer and Mass that was advertised as bilingual, but was in fact entirely in Spanish.[2] She would return either crying or just embarrassed—"I didn't know when to stand, when to sit, or what to say"—but then the next morning she would go back again.

I was watching all of this with only partial attention. I did not at all object, and I was interested to hear Amy's reports of what she was learning. But my mind was preoccupied with starting a 24-7 house of prayer in Austin, so I wasn't really paying attention as I should have been. One day in early 2000, I was driving down the road when suddenly the vivid thought came into my mind: "Amy wants to become Catholic."

Really?

This would explain a lot!

---

2 In addition to daily Mass each weekday morning, Cristo Rey was running nine weekend masses at that time. Their membership of close to ten thousand would have earned them the title of "megachurch" in the Protestant world, requiring a staff of dozens of pastors. But at Cristo Rey, the two Franciscan priests did all the work, with the assistance of four Salesian nuns. It was definitely eye-opening to see this huge work of God that was completely hidden from the Protestant pastors in the city.

When I arrived home, I asked Amy, "Do you want to become Catholic?"

"Oh, yes!" Amy replied. "There's nothing I want more. I love Hope Chapel, but now I am experiencing the presence of God most strongly at Cristo Rey. I think God is inviting me to become Catholic."

"But," she added, "I would never do anything that you could not bless with your whole heart."

Could I bless this with my whole heart? Not initially. If Amy were to become Catholic, it would affect our marriage, our children, our church life, our ministry, the potential house of prayer—everything! We began to talk, pray, and study together. We knew God was drawing Amy. But into what? We didn't have peace about her taking the huge step of becoming Catholic ... yet. We didn't want to make a hasty decision. We wanted to hear the Lord, with certainty, together.

And we did, in Switzerland. One day during our bathtub-inspired trip, we drove northwest to a small, out-of-the-way village called Romainmôtier. Back in Austin, Dan Davis's wife, Joann, had received a vision of Amy in that village's church. So we decided to go there to see what would happen.

The church in Romainmôtier. Photo by Thomas Cogdell.

We wandered in. We had the simple, quiet centuries-old church to ourselves. Amy walked down the aisle and turned into a side chapel to pray. I began the very holy activity of taking pictures. After a while, we both sensed it was time to go and walked out. As we settled into our rental car, we turned to each other and said—"It's OK. God is saying yes."

What happened in that church? Nothing spectacular—no vision, no dream, no audible voice of God. We didn't even pray together, that I remember. Yet somehow, God chose that time and place to give us both peace about the decision we were facing.

Sometimes the voice of God is powerful, shaking the cedars of Lebanon.

Sometimes the voice of God is small and subtle, barely discernible.

Always, the voice of God is greatly to be desired.

Amy and I had determined to not make a decision until we knew that we had heard the Lord together. And we heard the Lord in Romainmôtier, Switzerland.

Amy was going to become Catholic.

Use the QR code or visit **https://bit.ly/w17ch05** to explore more pictures and additional material for this chapter, including an amazing photo of Calvin's church in Geneva, Switzerland, with the floor removed.

Chapter 6

"The Guts to Go Through with It"

Wittenberg 2017 was not a gathering that went by; it brought FRUIT! Along the years-long process, it brought awareness to, and triggered a lot of repentance and reconciliation in, my own nation. During the gatherings, bondage was released, bridges were built, and relationships were established that made a difference.

In 2017, Austrians became friends with "Bruderhof"-people (Anabaptist background) and stayed in contact; two years later, we have a Bruderhof-community living near Vienna on property of the Dominican Order, given to them by the Vienna Roman Catholic archbishop; in the sixteenth century, their forefathers had been burned and drowned in Vienna by the same church.

GABRIELA SCHUBERT, Roman Catholic, founder of Mercy House of
Prayer, member of the Austrian Round Table, Vienna, Austria

Wittenberg—the very mention of the town's name brings a cascade of emotion for me. It was a time that brought focus and meaning to the past as well as direction for my journey into the future. I'm embracing my contemplative nature, and I'm experiencing a richer than ever intimacy with my Father and Friend. Thanks is inadequate.

ELIZABETH HUSS, Protestant / nondenominational, Austin, Texas
USA, widow of a direct descendant of Jan Hus

On the way from Switzerland to Paris to catch our flight back to the United States, we stopped by Taizé. This French community is best known in the States for its music and liturgy of prayer—you will often see something like "7:00 PM Taizé prayer service" advertised on church billboards.

But the heart of Taizé is reconciliation. It was founded after World War II by a Swiss Reformed Protestant. Brother Roger Schütz's first action was to invite Catholics to join—a bold move! Today it is a monastic order recognized by the Vatican, respected by Christians in Europe and around the world, and visited by hundreds of thousands every year.

In my mind, I pictured a pristine, quiet European monastery. I was looking forward to green lawns, old stone buildings, tinkling fountains, and profoundly deep worship times. The disappointing reality was more like Woodstock—hot, crowded, with buses of youth in various stages of dress (or undress) pulling in and out, battered guitars slung over their shoulders. I found the prayer times uninspiring. Maybe I was just tired at the end of our trip.

An important aspect of prayer at Taizé is an extended time of silence. During one of these times, I heard Amy whisper to me, "Thomas!" She said it in a voice that I knew well, which meant "I've got something that I'm really excited about, that I want to tell you!" I thought whatever it was that Amy was going to tell me must indeed be really important, because it was unlike Amy to break the rule of silence. But when I looked at her to hear it—she had turned away and was back to obeying prayerful silence.

That night before bed, I asked her what she wanted to tell me that was so important. "I didn't say anything to you, Thomas" was her reply. Slowly the realization settled over both of us—God had spoken to me during prayer. Audibly. This was not the "internal voice of the Spirit" that I was familiar with. It had been, without question, audible.

> God had spoken to me during prayer. Audibly.

What did it mean?

As we considered this short message, we began to uncover layer after layer of meaning. We thanked and praised God there in our room. We were astounded that he could speak so much in only one word. For me, the bottom line was that God was saying this: "When your wife is excited about something, *pay attention*—it's *me* speaking." And Amy was very excited about becoming Catholic!

We had made an appointment to meet with a monk at Taizé. He was not as excited about Amy becoming Catholic. Not that he was against it—far from it. He was simply nonplussed. He heard our story, and our breathless conclusion—"We think Amy should become Catholic, but I should remain Protestant." We waited for some sort of dramatic response. But he simply said, "Yes, that's not so unusual." It was a good perspective to hear, that for some this would be a normal way of life. Just because in our limited experience we had never encountered a Catholic–Protestant marriage didn't mean they didn't exist. Some humility was in order. We weren't making church history!

When we arrived back in Austin, we did something that—in retrospect—was very wise. We requested a meeting with Dan Davis, whom you will remember is the founding pastor of Hope Chapel.

Over pie at Marie Callender's, we told Dan the story of the past few years, up to our recent trip to Switzerland. We ended with this:

"You've always said there was only one church in the city. Well, we think God is calling Amy to become Catholic. And we want you to publicly bless this."

We knew that this move could be perceived as questionable or even offensive to some of the pastors in the city, many of whom we were working with in the house of prayer. But if we had the visible blessing of the founder of Hope Chapel, who was highly regarded as a father figure by many of these same pastors … well, that would be different.

Dan's reply surprised us.

"Sure, I can bless this. But I don't think you've got the guts to go through with it!"

The response of Father Larry, the priest at Cristo Rey, also surprised us—but for a different reason.

"Oh, please don't do that," he said when Amy announced to him that she was going to become Catholic. Why did he say this? He explained that had seen too many families divided, and he didn't want our marriage to be threatened.

How many Protestant pastors would respond the same way, if a Catholic woman came to them and said, "I want to join your church"? The typical response would be, "Great! And bring your husband along too." Protestant churches often have an unhealthy focus on attendance and membership numbers. I don't find this in nearly the same degree in the Catholic churches that I have had experience with. We Protestants can learn from our Catholic brothers and sisters—numbers don't validate the existence of the church.

Amy set up a meeting between me and Father Larry. Even I could tell that he was nervous. I suspect he thought I would accuse him of stealing my wife away. I tried to assure him that Amy and I were in agreement on this decision, willing to embrace a life of reconciliation.

> We Protestants can learn from our Catholic brothers and sisters—numbers don't validate the existence of the church.

Finally, he gave in and told Amy: "Well, I can't stop you from becoming Catholic. But if you do, then I am your priest and have some authority to speak into your life. And my charge to you is this: When you become Catholic, you must come to Mass every week—as every Catholic is required to do. But you must also continue to attend Hope Chapel every Sunday with your family. And I would suggest that they attend Mass with you, every month or two—so that you have a shared experience as a family, not a divided one." What a wise man!

And this is the way that Amy and I have lived ever since Easter Sunday of 2001, when she officially became a member of the Roman Catholic Church.

Our family on a missions trip to Mexico with the Cristo Rey youth group, including Sister Guadalupe, in her habit (left); Jack Salazar (top right), with his wife, Yolanda; Nina from the dream is holding our son Justus, with Peggy and Noah in front of her. Photo by Thomas Cogdell.

There is one more part of the trip to Switzerland in the year 2000 that must be told.

My father had given us a complete set of Will and Ariel Durant's *Story of Civilization*. On the way to the airport, we grabbed *Volume 6, The Reformation*. We wanted to learn more about how the Protestants originally split off from the Catholic Church. Some might question the romance of carrying this heavy tome on our anniversary trip!

As we sat on our patio in Huémoz, eating Swiss chocolate and reading German history, my attention was suddenly captured by this:

The date for the Reformation was October 31, 1517.

"Wow, the 500th anniversary is going to be in my lifetime," I thought. "What are the odds of that, that such a significant anniversary would be within reach?"

On the flight back, I turned to Amy and said, "You know, it would be good if there were a meeting in Wittenberg in 2017, where Protestants and Catholics gathered on the 500th anniversary to grieve their division, and pray John 17 together."

"Yes," she replied, "that's a great idea."

"Maybe it's up to us to make this happen," I mused.

"Thomas, we are two laypeople in Austin, Texas. We can't organize an international prayer meeting!"

I agreed and leaned back in my airplane seat, trying to make myself comfortable for the long flight ahead of us. The number 7 came into my mind. "Maybe, in seven years, I'll travel to Wittenberg and reserve a room for 2017 … ," I thought, as I drifted off to sleep.

Use the QR code or visit **https://bit.ly/w17ch06** to explore more pictures and additional material for this chapter, including a picture of Father Larry from Cristo Rey.

Part II

Testing, 2001–2010

Waiting

I have been part of an Anabaptist mission for the past twenty years to see healing experienced in issues of our Reformation history. Our focus for the past fifteen years has been to see healing with the Catholics related to the Anabaptist responsibility for the 1531–34 atrocity in Münster, Germany. This mission was at a standstill until some connections with Prince Michael Salm at Wittenberg 2017. The Lord had given me a word in 2007 that Prince Michael had the key to help open the door for this healing. The Holy Spirit resurrected this calling on Michael ten years later at the conference, and he helped open the way for an amazing reconciliation event in Münster in May 2018. The Lord showed us that as a result of the Anabaptists' misrepresentation of the Holy Spirit and the spiritual gifts in Münster, the Catholic Church and the Reformation parties were all affected with a fear of becoming too open to the Holy Spirit. As a result, the apostolic and prophetic gifts were basically silenced for the next 400 years. We are believing that this fear is losing its power over all of the Reformation parties.

> LLOYD HOOVER, bishop, Lancaster Mennonite Conference
> (Anabaptist), Lancaster, Pennsylvania USA

I echo [Amish leader] Ben Girod's words: the Wittenberg 2017 leadership team has led all the meetings, and especially this very large last one, with unprecedented grace and humility. Beauty being something I think we humans crave (at least I do), I'm very privileged to have witnessed such beauty these many years. Thank you, Lord. Thank you, Thomas and Amy.

> SANDI PEDROTTI, Hope Chapel (Protestant / nondenominational),
> Christ the Reconciler Community, Austin, Texas USA

Seven years from the year 2000 would be 2007. So for seven years, Amy and I waited.[1]

---

1 When I had the inner sense of the number "7" in the year 2000 and interpreted it as "going to Wittenberg in seven years to reserve a room" (see the end of chapter 6), I didn't think of any possibility other than my traveling to Wittenberg personally. It never occurred to me that we could try to contact any hotel or reach out to get information remotely about conference rooms in Wittenberg, or have one of our friends in Germany act as an agent to explore the options. This oversight was surely providential. "Who is blind like … the servant of the Lord?" (Isa 42:19).

Simply waiting has a rich biblical heritage. Abraham waited for Isaac—somewhat impatiently, of course. Moses waited for Pharoah to let God's people go. Anointed king by Samuel in his youth, David waited until Saul's death to actually become king—and refused to hasten the process, even when provided the opportunity.

Jesus practiced carpentry until the right time to begin his ministry, then continually waited on his Father's word for each action. The disciples waited with Mary in the upper room for they-knew-not-what. Paul waited in Tarsus for thirteen years.

The followers of Jesus have been waiting for millennia for the return of the Messiah in glory.

So seven years is not too long to wait.

During these years, the vision of Wittenberg 2017 remained in our minds—but in the back of them, not the front.

Peggy and Justus inspect their new brother, John Patrick. Photo by Thomas Cogdell.

In the front of our minds were many other things. We now had four children. Noah and Peggy were growing up. Justus had been added in 1999, and Amy gave birth to John Patrick in 2003.

Life was filled with sibling squabbles. Unexpected house repairs would break in at the worst moments—I remember crouching in a fierce winter rainstorm, cold water pouring down my back while I tried desperately to relight the water heater pilot. And most agonizing of all, just when we would fall asleep at the end of another long day, the dreaded sound would start—John Patrick awake and crying in his crib. "Isn't it your turn this time, honey?" Of course, there were also many moments of joy and laughter, but these were some of the hardest years of our marriage.

To any young parents reading this book—please know that this, too, will pass. And if you endure, you will emerge from the other side transformed into a better human being. As Oliver Wendell Holmes Jr. said, "I would not give a fig for the simplicity this side of complexity, but I would give my life for the simplicity on the other side of complexity."

Amy was in the midst of complexity during these seven years of waiting. She was a wife to a difficult husband (more on that in the next chapter). She was a homeschooling teacher, not only of her own children but of others as well. She was already being sought out by many as a confidant and counselor. In other words, she was a superhero.[2]

There were also consolations among the complexities.

Amy was learning to love the rhythm of life as a new Catholic. Amy's friendship with Caroline Owens was growing ever deeper and more rewarding. Phillip and Caroline became Catholic a few years after Amy—for their own reasons, which perhaps they'll write into their own book someday. Now Amy could receive the Eucharist with her dear friend.

I was working closely with Phillip as well, on the 24-7 prayer project. Our name for it was Austin House of Prayer, or AHOP for short. We found others who were allies in the cause of day-and-night prayer and began to work together to see it become a reality in Austin.

I learned so much during those early AHOP days. First and foremost was that scripture records amazing prayers. It's one thing to know they are there, it's another to take these prayers into your heart and make them your own. And that is what I began to do—the hymns of Revelation, the apostolic prayers of Paul, the prayers of Jesus, Moses, David, and Jonah. The more I prayed each one, the deeper it became, and the easier to pray. What a treasure!

It was the International House of Prayer (IHOP) in Kansas City that taught us about biblical prayers. IHOP was born out of the Metro Christian Fellowship church that we had discovered in the late nineties. IHOP had developed a new model of blending musical worship and prayer. The musician or musical team continues to play instrumentally in the background when the time for prayer comes. Then singers sing the prayers that the prayer leader is praying. The emphasis is on short prayers from Scripture.[3] The ancient word "antiphonal" captures the back-and-forth nature between the prayer leader and the singers.

---

2 Amy and I really love the movie *The Incredibles*, especially the scene where Elastigirl and her two kids are in the ocean after their plane crashes, and she says to them, "I tell you what we're not going to do, we're not going to panic ... Now, both of you will *get a grip*! Or so help me, I will ground you for a month. Understand?" All mothers are superheroes. Especially Amy.

3 Rather than long prayers from one's imagination—which of course can also be fine and good.

The growth in my prayer life was exhilarating. Before, a two-hour prayer session would have been unthinkable—agonizingly boring. Now I entered in with anticipation. Over the course of two hours, my mind would be exploding—connecting scripture to scripture, imagining the scene around the throne of God, passionately interceding for the church worldwide, and coordinating a team of musicians, singers, and other intercessors. When the prayer time came to an end, I would have more energy than I started with. I was addicted.

Soon we had an entire day of the week covered in prayer, and a talented and dedicated group of college students and young adults were doing a "night watch" from midnight Friday through to 6:00 AM Saturday morning.

Our worlds were already starting to collide. Here we invited the Cristo Rey youth group, led by Jack Salazar and Sister Guadalupe, to join us in a night watch session in a pop-up house of prayer on the campus of the University of Texas. Amy is on the left and Peggy is in the center, holding John Patrick. Photo by Thomas Cogdell.

During this time, I was enjoying my paying job as well. Since 1998, I have worked for an Austin-based consulting firm named Athens Group. Consulting fits my personality well—solve one client's problem, then move on to the next project, without having to worry about long-term management and maintenance. My assignments in the mid-2000s were almost all close to home. I worked on successful projects at the corporate headquarters of Dell, Whole Foods Market, and Keller Williams Realty. Athens Group had been founded as an employee-centered company, so I was allowed to set my own work schedule. Whenever I got a raise, I would cut my hours proportionately, in order to keep my pay the same but free up more time in the prayer room.

And through all of this, in the back of my mind, lingered the vision of a prayer meeting for Catholics and Protestants in Wittenberg on the 500th anniversary … Wittenberg 2017.

 Use the QR code or visit https://bit.ly/w17ch07 to explore more pictures and additional material for this chapter, including a video of Phillip leading the best Psalm 23 worship song you have never heard of, with a description of its connection to the Owens becoming Catholic *and* my salvation at the age of seven, plus a bonus appearance by Steve Hawthorne.

It all came to a head, curiously enough, not with a major decision involving tens of thousands of dollars, but with something seemingly small and relatively insignificant.[2] Isn't this how it usually is? The deep pains are stored up, and then the smallest pinprick causes a massive eruption.

The pinprick that would burst open Amy's wounds began with a Sunday morning announcement early in the spring of 2003. The arts pastor of Hope Chapel invited members of the church to participate in creating a new art exhibit that would be unveiled on Easter morning.[3] The theme of the art exhibit was the six days of creation, with each day represented by a large four-by-eight panel that would be hung on the walls of the church. He needed a leader for each panel, and a group of volunteers of all ages to help create the artworks.

His announcement immediately sparked an idea for the second day of creation, where water was separated from water, revealing the sky. I saw in my mind's eye the finger of God touching down and the water rolling back—and the finger of God was a mirror, that also looked like a whirlwind or tornado.

Well, if you've made it this far in the book, you have undoubtedly learned a few things about my personality. First of all, I really like ideas. God has given some people the gift of being able to easily generate ideas, and I have always had this capability.

Second of all, I love projects. Starting a new project is my cup of tea. God has gifted me with the ability to communicate vision, assemble a team, and know intuitively the first steps to take to get the ball rolling.

A third part of my personality may not have been apparent yet. I am secretly a wannabe artist. I am a very visual thinker, and many of my ideas—like this one for the art panel—come to me as images. I sometimes am jealous of all the wonderful artists whose art hangs on the walls of Hope Chapel. I long to see people gaze thoughtfully at *my* work of art, then turn to engage *me* in discussion about the deep layers of meaning they are discovering.

---

2 Though I did in fact conceal some of those high-stakes financial decisions from Amy, too.

3 The arts pastor at Hope Chapel in those days was W. David O. Taylor. David is now an Anglican priest and professor at Fuller Seminary. He has written several books about the arts (https://www.wdavidotaylor.com/). His most recent book is *Open and Unafraid: The Psalms as a Guide to Life*, co-written with Eugene Peterson—whom David famously interviewed together with Bono in a 2016 short film.

All three of these aspects of my personality were activated that fateful Sunday morning. I felt something rising up in me, driving me to sign up for the second panel. As the service went on, I irrationally began to be afraid that someone else would seize it before I had a chance. I wondered if I should sneak over during the sermon and tell the arts pastor, "Day two is mine!" ... but I nobly restrained myself. As soon as the service was over, I rushed over and signed up to be the leader for Easter Art Panel #2. Whew, nobody else had asked for it yet! I was given a team of volunteers and a budget for materials, and we would all assemble on a Saturday morning in April to create the art panel.

So far, so good. The only problem was ... I didn't tell Amy I had done this.

Why didn't I tell Amy? Why hadn't I told her about AHOP three years earlier? Why do any of us do the things that we do? Have you ever done something, then wondered, "Why did I just do that?" That is a question rarely asked ... and when asked, usually brushed aside.

I have come to name this internal drive, my *compulsions*. Other words such as "addiction" could be substituted here, but I like the word compulsion, for reasons I will unfold later. I was *compelled* to sign up for the Easter art project. It was like there was a little ball of nervous energy, sitting in my stomach, driving me to do it.

Do you know this feeling? There's a sense in which, at the time, I had no choice. I was the kind of person who could not resist his compulsions. I had to sign up.

Right beside that little ball of nervous energy was a companion, a little ball of secret fear. This fear prevented me from telling Amy about my commitment. I call this fear a compulsion, as well. But it's more of a negative one. Rather than compelling me to take action, it compelled me to be passive—to *not* do something I knew I should do.

Years later I became aware of a passage in 1 Samuel 13 about Saul's compulsions and the damage they caused to him, his family, and the nation of Israel. Saul is tall and handsome. He has been chosen by God to be the first king of Israel, and Samuel has anointed him with oil. He has won initial victories. But then comes the Philistine army, "as numerous as the sand on the seashore." Saul's men are afraid and begin to slip away in the night. As his army dwindles, Saul is waiting for Samuel to arrive and offer the necessary sacrifice. Samuel fails to show up, and Saul makes his fatal mistake—he offers the sacrifice himself.

Why does he do this? As Saul says in 1 Samuel:

> "When I saw that the men were scattering, and that you did not come at the set time, and that the Philistines were assembling at Mikmash, I thought, 'Now the Philistines will come down against me at Gilgal, and I have not sought the LORD's favor.' *So I felt compelled to offer the burnt offering.*"

> "You acted foolishly," Samuel said. "You have not kept the command the LORD your God gave you; if you had, he would have established your kingdom over Israel for all time. But now your kingdom will not endure; the LORD has sought out a man after his own heart and appointed him leader of his people, because you have not kept the LORD's command." (1 Sam 13:11–14; emphasis added)

Now as we all know, the man after God's own heart was David. David had his own problems. He was impulsive. But he was not compulsive. Impulsive behaviors are onetime events. Compulsions repeat themselves in a person's life.

At Gilgal, Saul was afraid of his army deserting him. He felt compelled to act. I recognize myself in this passage. I suspect that Saul had that same ball of nerves in the pit of his stomach, that same impatience that grew day by day, the same hidden fear of being exposed and ridiculed. His compulsions finally drove him to supplant Samuel as priest.

God's judgment on this action is clear. God does not overlook Saul's compulsive sins. The compulsions of leaders can cause great damage because they influence many people. Saul's compulsions eventually disqualify him from leadership. God's anointing passes to another.

Would God overlook my compulsive sins? Would I be able to hide from Amy that I had signed up to spend an entire Saturday creating an art panel? Of course not! I had that inching-closer-to-the-edge-of-the-cliff dread of the inevitable moment I would have to tell her.

And rightly so. It did not go well when I casually mentioned to her, "Oh, by the way, Amy ... I'm in charge of creating one of the art panels for Hope Chapel, so I won't be here on Saturday." I had strategically waited long enough to tell her, that I thought she couldn't say no. After all, if I wasn't there, who else could create Art Panel #2? And how could you not have day two of creation? The birds created on day five would have no place to fly if there were no sky from day two!

Well, Amy didn't share my view of the importance of the second day of creation. Can you believe, she actually asked me to not do it! When she pleaded with me to not leave her alone with our four kids for a whole day on the weekend, after she had cared for them all week while I was at work, part of me felt bad. I briefly considered letting the pastor know I couldn't be there. But then a new compulsion kicked in—I didn't want to let him down.[4] So I ratcheted up the pressure on Amy to let me do it.

First, I justified myself by explaining that this was for Hope Chapel … ultimately, it was for the glory of God that I was going to be gone on Saturday. Second, I negotiated with her by promising to take Noah and Peggy with me to help on the project … so that she would "only" have the two youngest to care for.[5]

I finally put enough pressure on her that she gave in. "OK," she relented, "but please come home as quickly as possible." Inside, my emotions were complex. My compulsion to lead and create was satisfied, which felt good. But there was a sorrow mixed in. Deep inside I knew I had damaged my wife—first by not telling her, then by forcing her to submit to what I wanted to do.

Well … it gets worse.

The fateful Saturday arrived, and Hope Chapel was abuzz with six teams creating the six days of creation. Ours went well, and the basic board was done when everyone else stopped, around noon. Amy called to ask if I was coming home, and I said yes, I was just about to leave.

This was a lie. I actually was not about to leave. My vision for the panel was not yet complete. In my mind's eye, there was a frame of copper pipes around our board. And little clear stickers on the pipes with scriptures about water printed on them. "It would just take a few minutes," I justified to myself, without telling Amy of my plans.

---

4 Sadly, I didn't have a compulsion to not let *Amy* down …

5 Those are deadly words: justify, negotiate. Many marriages consist of a lot of justification, and a lot of negotiation. When God speaks in scripture about the holy unity of marriage, justification and negotiation are not what he has in mind. There is no self-justification or negotiation in the Trinity.

I created the stickers on my computer. I printed them out. I began trying to put the stickers on the pipes. It wasn't as easy in reality as it had seemed in my imagination.

I ruined one set of stickers, and started printing a second set. An hour passed by … then two. Noah and Peggy were asking, "Daddy, when are we going to leave?" "In a minute, kids." Of course, a minute to a parent is like a thousand years to a child.

Finally, there was the dreaded call from Amy—"Where *are* you?" I didn't have a choice. I had to explain about the pipes and stickers. She couldn't believe it. She strongly "encouraged" me that the stickers were *not* necessary. But I just couldn't let it go. Like Saul, I was compelled.

We finally headed home around 4:00 PM.

Wrath. That is the only word to describe the mood Amy was in when I got home. I had never seen her like this before. I became immediately defensive and snapped back at her. This was the one and only time in our marriage that we were so loud, the house became somewhat confining. So we moved our argument to the backyard. She was screaming at me, "You didn't need the dumb stickers!" and I was screaming back, "The stickers were important!"

Then, it got worse.

You see, I had also committed to be at an AHOP prayer meeting at 5:00 PM. And I hadn't told Amy about that either. So, as the backyard argument was progressing, I was sneaking sideways glances at the time. When I tried to excuse myself from the fixed glare of my wife by telling her I had to go to this prayer meeting, Amy lost it. "What?!! You have got to be kidding me!"

Then she looked at me with great pain in her eyes and said the last thing that I expected: "I'm yelling at you because I love you! Don't you know that I am for you, not against you?"

> I'm yelling at you because I love you!

This stunned me. It went right around all of the defensive arguments I had lined up. A glimmer of hope appeared in my dark heart. Amy was for me? She wasn't against me?

"Really?" I stammered.

"Yes, of course!" Amy responded. "I like your ideas. I like the things you make. I want you to pursue your visions. I am really happy that you want to pray. I work hard so that you can do all these things."

Something about the gentle, pleading way that Amy said this got through to me. You see, Amy saw the compulsions in me, but that was not all that she saw. She saw deeper. By the power of the Holy Spirit, she saw the pain in me that fed those compulsions. She could have used this insight against me—to wound me or to manipulate me. Instead, she directly addressed my pain with her love. I will ever be grateful to Amy for what she said that afternoon in the backyard.

Her words began a healing process in me.

During this season of healing, Amy had a dream in which she saw this painting of my heart being purified by God. An amazing artist friend of ours, James B. Janknegt, painted it based on her description from the dream. Photo by Thomas Cogdell. Used with permission from James B. Janknegt. See https://www.bcartfarm.com for more of James's paintings.

It was a good thing that my period of waiting was seven years, because the healing process took the last several—and in many ways is still ongoing, fifteen years later. But the first step happened quickly.

I became acutely aware of my compulsions.

I was unable to resist them, true, but I was no longer blind to them. I was placed in situation after situation where my compulsions drove me to do what I did not want to do. Each time, my eyes were opened to my sinfulness. Instead of reacting with defensiveness, with fear, with justification, with negotiation … I was sorrowful, repented, and pledged that next time would be different. And next time. And next time. And through it all, Amy patiently endured.

During this difficult season, the Holy Spirit highlighted a phrase from 2 Corinthians 5:14. It is part of a passage written by the apostle Paul about his own ministry.

For Christ's love compels us …

Paul was also aware of his compulsions … but his compulsions were pure! Compelled by the love of Christ … could this be possible? Could I reach a place where my damaging compulsions would be replaced by a godly compulsion? Could I, too, become compelled by Christ's love?

This became my prayer all those years ago, and has been with me ever since.

It has been a great encouragement to me that it was Paul who penned this phrase. After all, Paul was also named Saul. Remember King Saul's compulsions—the ones that disqualified him from kingship? Saul of Tarsus was once just like that—compelled by everything except the love of Christ. In fact, he was compelled by hatred of Jesus to destroy the church. Yet God intervened in Saul's life and changed his compulsions. Twenty years later, as he wrote his second letter to the Corinthians, he had been transformed. His only compulsion is the love of Christ.

This is cause for great hope. Our unhealthy compulsions *can* be diminished and ultimately removed. We *can* come to the place where we no longer need to hide them, or to justify them, or to negotiate our way around them.

> This is cause for great hope. Our unhealthy compulsions *can* be diminished and ultimately removed.

Over the years—2004, 2005, 2006, into 2007—I became increasingly able to see my compulsions. And not only see them, but repent from them. And not only repent from them, but renounce them. My Saul-like compulsions began diminishing. Sin was losing its grip on me.

I am now convinced that Wittenberg 2017 would not have happened without this time of testing and refining in my heart. Or perhaps God would have chosen other leaders, and we would have watched from afar. If I had carried my compulsive leadership patterns into a global initiative for reconciliation and unity, surely chaos and disaster would have ensued. The damage would have been extensive. I am so thankful to the Lord for doing the work that David prayed for in Psalm 139:

Search me, God, and know my heart;
    test me and know my anxious thoughts.
See if there is any offensive way in me,
    and lead me in the way everlasting.

I had prayed this biblical prayer many times in the AHOP prayer room. I had no idea what I was asking for! Even so, the Lord heard my prayer and answered. I am thankful for this. Amy and many other friends were also praying fervently for me during this season of testing.

Recently, Amy has told me why she didn't say no to the vision of the house of prayer, even though she saw clearly that I was not pursuing it in a healthy, mature manner. We were in our early thirties at the time. Amy determined that she would rather my compulsions be directed toward a godly end than toward other options. She had seen many men in their "boring forties" go off the rails into adultery, addiction, abandonment, and a litany of other woes.

Oh, the wisdom of this woman! I am so deeply grateful to the Lord for her, and for our marriage.

And Amy was right. I have never felt dissatisfied with my life. Our life has not been boring. Not at all. More like a rollercoaster. And the season of waiting and testing was like the jerky climb up the first big hill …

"Buckle your seatbelts, and keep your arms and legs inside the vehicle at all times!"

Use the QR code or visit **https://bit.ly/w17ch08** to explore more pictures and additional material for this chapter, including an amazing fact about Jim Janknegt paired with a full-color photo of his painting.

Chapter 9

"Let Me Do It"

While much time has passed since the gathering in Wittenberg, I do recall the time fondly. I was especially touched by acts of reconciliation between the Anabaptist and Lutheran streams as well as the presence of the Roman Catholic bishop. The march through the streets of Wittenberg will always remain with me as well.

JAMES BREDESON, senior pastor of Victory Lutheran Church, Medicine Hat, Alberta, Canada

For me, the idea of unity and its realization is something that has since shaped my spiritual life and my work in the church. In Wittenberg 2017, I experienced a unity across denominations, generations, national borders, and cultures—and that without anyone being required to give up their denominational, generational, national, or cultural identity. What brings us together in unity is Jesus himself. For this reason, I perceive the differences as enriching—in the sense of 1 Corinthians 12, the image of the body.

The thought that won't let go of me lately is the question of how a community of Christians who live in the same area see themselves as responsible for this area or city. In a major city, of course, this looks different than it does in a small town like Eimeldingen, where we live. Many Christians drive to the neighboring village to live out community, and hardly know any fellow Christians in their immediate area. Would their task be to live out Christian community in their local neighborhood, where they really are "home" in other respects? How can we live out Christian unity in our own immediate neighborhood?

The idea of reconciliation has also become increasingly important to me. This work of the Holy Spirit brings us back from our own preconceptions and preferences to Jesus. And to our Jewish roots. Back to the people of God.

JOCHEN DEBUS, pastor, Evangelical Lutheran Church, Eimeldingen, Germany

The year 2007 came … and I wondered if I would be going to Germany to reserve a room in Wittenberg.

I had waited seven years. Now I continued to wait. I was waiting for God. I knew I could have taken initiative myself and arranged my own travel to Germany. But the idea of doing that just felt wrong to my spirit. Besides, I was busy with other things.

In addition to the house of prayer, we had started a bottled-water business called Cielo. The purpose of the business was to provide funds for the house of prayer project.[1] But of course the early days of starting a business involve putting money in, not getting money out. I was writing business plans, seeking investors, putting together a startup team, and watching the business get off the ground.

We had also sold the Canterbury house and moved into a new house on Martin Luther King Jr. Blvd. The MLK house had a smaller house in the back, which is why we bought it. The term "mother-in-law house" was literally true for us. Amy's stepfather had died, and her mother, Geri, was significantly disabled and unable to live on her own. So now we were living together, and the kids ran constantly from our back door, to her front door, and back—stopping regularly to jump on the trampoline in between.

I wasn't in danger of becoming bored.

And so when the year 2007 had passed, I had not gone to Germany.

I put the Wittenberg 2017 idea aside as just that, only an idea—not from God, but from my own imagination. This didn't trouble me much. I had many other irons in the fire.

A few months into 2008, our former youth pastor Jayson Knox called. "I want to invite you guys to an Antioch Network meeting this summer. It's in Herrnhut, Germany."

Herrnhut! For anybody interested in 24-7 prayer, that name stirs interest and desire. Herrnhut is the site of the "100-Year Prayer Meeting," which ran 24-7 for more than 130 years! The Moravian community that lived there also pioneered the modern Protestant missions movement.

How could we not go to Herrnhut?

---

1 This type of business has since become more prevalent, given the name "social venture"— or in the church, "business as mission" (BAM).

We talked about making a family vacation out of the trip. Noah would be graduating from high school in a few years, so this was perhaps our last chance to include him in an overseas trip. We decided to use Herrnhut as an anchor, but travel all through Europe before and afterward. We told our children, "We have to show up in Herrnhut, but we don't want your memory of Europe to be a boring Christian meeting. So just tell us when you're ready to go, and we'll leave early."[2]

The plans were set, and we packed our duffel bags with tents and sleeping bags. We couldn't afford to stay in hotels all three weeks, and we had heard that campgrounds in Europe were much nicer than in the United States. I had reserved a rental "minivan" online—imagining a spacious American vehicle easily seating the six of us, with plenty of room in the back and a luggage rack on top.

When we landed in Berlin, we rolled our carts with more than a dozen suitcases, duffel bags, and backpacks up to the rental car counter. The agent stared in disbelief: "You will not fit in this car."

I stared back. "Just give me the key."

Once in the parking garage, Amy and the four kids groaned in dismay. To describe our vehicle as a "small hatchback" would have been generous. I responded with my usual optimism—"We can do it!" And we eventually did. Luggage was packed beneath, around, and on top of us as we drove to our Berlin hotel.

Our "minivan" with the duffel bags roped on top. Photo by Thomas Cogdell.

The next morning everyone was groggy except for me—I usually don't suffer from jet lag. We bought a rope and tied the three duffel bags with camping gear on top of the car.

This freed up a little more room inside, though it also meant we had to keep the windows slightly open

---

2 To be honest, we were drawn much more by the location of Herrnhut than by the event of the Antioch Network gathering. From our last contact with Antioch Network in the 1990s, we remembered a mission organization mobilizing churches to send church-planting teams to unreached people groups. We were not at all opposed to this focus—after all, missions had been the originally-expected course of our lives. It was just that God had directed the river of our hearts into prayer and reconciliation. (The Antioch Network vision and history can be found at https://www.antioch-network.org.)

for the rope to pass through the inside of the car. Fortunately the German climate we arrived in was much nicer than the Texas heat we had left behind.

We headed south out of Berlin toward our first stop. It would take about six hours to drive to Rothenburg ob der Tauber, a medieval village that had miraculously escaped bombing during World War II. Once we reached "Die Autobahn," I began to experiment with increasing my speed—until I noticed that the wind was getting under the duffel bags on top, threatening to rip them off altogether! So it was back to the far right lane for us, as Audis and BMWs sped deliciously past on the left.

Amy and the children were soon asleep. I was now on the A9 highway, about an hour out of Berlin.

Suddenly, I noticed the sign: *Wittenberg, next exit.*

What?!

Noah had purchased a cheap digital camera for the trip, and recorded this picture from the back seat of me driving on the Autobahn. Photo by Noah Cogdell.

I snapped fully awake, my mind racing. I hadn't considered the possibility that Wittenberg would be on our way. "I can reserve the room for 2017, after all!" Immediately I planned to take the exit. "2008 is pretty close to 2007," I thought, "and maybe God's math was just a little fuzzy."

Then I looked at my lovely wife, asleep in the front seat next to me. I considered the fact that I was about to wreck our carefully planned schedule, before we'd even been in Europe one whole day. She would not be pleased.

And the children. They were expecting to wake up at the Museum of Medieval Weaponry in Rothenburg. Waking up to a search for meeting rooms in Wittenberg would not be a welcome substitute.

What to do? I had only a few seconds to make a decision. So I prayed.

Lord, should I take the exit, or not?

Immediately, I heard a clear response.

You can take the exit … and it will be you. Or, you can pass it by, and let me do it.

So I settled my hands at the top of the steering wheel and kept the car pointed straight ahead. The exit slipped past on the right, into my rearview mirror, then faded away behind us.

In one way, it was easy—because I had seen the damage my compulsions could cause. I knew that if anything of worth were to happen in Wittenberg, it would have to be God's doing.

But it was still one of the more courageous decisions I had ever made. I was a few minutes away from the place I had been thinking about for years. I had already let this dream die at the end of 2007. Now, five months later, I had seen it suddenly resurrected—only to immediately lay it back on the altar and kill it again.

My one hope was the last part of what I heard: "… let me do it." Perhaps God had a plan that I couldn't see. But when would I ever be near Wittenberg again?

Little did I know that in that moment Wittenberg 2017 was set into motion. By refusing to go to Wittenberg in my own strength, I had passed a critical test the Lord had set before me.

My mind whirred until Amy woke up. I told her what had happened, and she sleepily said, "I told you that Wittenberg would be on the way." Had she really? I'm sure she was right, but I had no memory of this.

I am so thankful that I didn't hear her then.[3] Given time to think about the decision, I certainly would have screwed it all up by arranging to visit Wittenberg.

And I am so thankful that I *had* heard her when she confronted me years before. God knew I had to crucify my compulsions before I reached that Autobahn exit to Wittenberg.

 Use the QR code or visit **https://bit.ly/w17ch09** to explore a map, more pictures, and additional material for this chapter, including what can happen when five strapping young men all jump on a trampoline at the same time.

---

3 Isaiah 42:19 again: "Who is … deaf like the messenger I send?"

Chapter 10

Herrnhut

Coming from an ecumenical international Christian community, it was very inspiring to see and hear others expressing their love for Christ and their desire for his Church to be made one.

The highlight for me was being in Martin Luther's church in Wittenberg, sitting in the ugliness and pain of the Judensau. We had a service led by various church leaders—Orthodox, Lutheran, Catholic. At the end, the KISI choir surrounded us in the sanctuary. They raised their hands and sang a blessing over us—first in Hebrew, then in English:

> "May the Lord bless you. May the Lord keep you safe. May the Lord shine His countenance upon you.
>
> May the Lord give you grace. May His glory shine through your face. May He be gracious to you."[1]

It was a sacred moment.

Dave and Jane Hughes, Presbyterian, Sword of the Spirit Community, Ann Arbor, Michigan USA

What an awesome, Holy Spirit–inspired movement of the unity of the body of Christ nationally and internationally. It took years of preparation and was mainly initiated by Thomas Cogdell, who has found favor with God and gathered a wide range of the body of Christ in Wittenberg on the occasion of the 500th anniversary of the Reformation by Martin Luther. Humility and repentance paved the way for these days of prayer, penance, and intercession for one another.

It was a privilege to participate and spiritually add to this event as the FCJG/HELP community. It was a significant time—especially for the nation of Germany—foremost because of the relationship between Germany and Israel as well as digging into Germany's spiritual history and relationship to the people of Israel. This movement was and is—as it continues in Germany—a milestone of what God still has in plan for us.

Walter Heidenreich, Pentecostal, founder and president of FCJG (Freie Christliche Jugend Gemeinschaft / Free Christian Youth Community) and HELP International, Lüdenscheid, Germany

---

1 Lyrics from *The Shema Israel*, part of the musical *The Covenant*, written by Elizabeth and Robert Muren, and used by KISI with their permission. For more about the KISI, see chapter 24 and visit https://www.kisi.org/en/.

Our itinerary for the first two weeks in Europe was ambitious. We landed in Germany and visited the medieval city of Rothenburg ob der Tauber. Then south into Switzerland for the mountains. From there we drove farther south into Italy. We stayed at Cinque Terre on the Mediterranean, then made our way inland. Each of the children was allowed to pick one place in Europe to visit. Justus, who loved St. Francis, chose the caves of La Verna, where Francis spent his last years. Peggy chose Venice. After Italy, we crossed the Austrian border and spent two days in Salzburg. Then finally back to Germany, with the nose of our car pointed toward Herrnhut.

Rick Steves's book on Europe was our guide. I followed his recommendations religiously, much to my family's amusement. When we arrived in Italy, I bought a newspaper at the first stop and tossed it into onto the dashboard.

"What is that for?" Amy asked.

"Oh," I explained earnestly, "Rick Steves says that in Italy, you should put a newspaper on your dashboard so thieves will think you're a local and leave your car alone."

Amy and the kids burst into laughter. Slowly, I began to see the ridiculousness of my actions. Any thief spying a car with German license plates, stuffed with luggage, and crowned with camping gear tied on top wasn't likely to be deceived by a local newspaper!

A more serious "father error" brought us some grief, though we now laugh about it. We had borrowed a large family tent for the trip. After our second night of use, I decided to give our eldest a lesson in camping. "Noah, let me teach you how to clean out a tent."

I lifted the entire empty tent over my head and began to shake it, causing the dirt, dust, and leaves to fall though the opening at the bottom. Suddenly there was a loud *snap*! The entire six-person tent collapsed around me. Upon investigation, we found that the plastic hub that held all the poles together had broken. I couldn't believe it. We had two weeks of camping ahead of us, and I had just broken the tent! From then on, at every campground, I had to sheepishly ask for a site with trees so we could suspend our tent from the tree branches with ropes. All I can say is … it worked. Mostly. Unless it rained.

Our children learned a lot about the different cultures of Europe. The evening we arrived in Switzerland was stressful. We got lost and feared we would be late to our campsite. We actually drove right by the campground just before 9:00 PM but missed the sign. Once we turned around and parked, it was slightly after nine. We were met at the gate by a stern-faced Swiss guardian of the campground.

"This campground is closed."

"But we're only a few minutes late!"

"The campground closed at 9:00 PM."

"But we were actually here before nine, we just missed the turn!"

"I am sorry, the campground is closed."

"But we've traveled all day and have nowhere else to go!"

"I cannot help you. This campground is closed."

Apparently Swiss campground guards are as punctual as the country's famous trains. We thought this was silly. We waited until he left his post at the gate, tossed our bags over the fence, walked through the open gate, set up in an empty spot, and went to sleep. The next morning, we went to the office to pay. The lady behind the counter looked up our name and campsite number.

"You were not here."

"No, we were here. We came in after the gate was closed."

"Impossible. You were not here."

"Can we just pay for our campsite?"

"No. I cannot accept your money. You were not here."

We got a free night of camping and a lesson in reality from the point of view of the Swiss.

Just a few days later, after getting hopelessly lost in Florence, we found ourselves once again late to our campground. Not just a few Swiss seconds late this time—we arrived several Italian hours after closing. We pulled up to the gate around midnight. There was only one light on in the gatehouse. Tentatively, I pushed the door open to find the elderly campground hosts drinking red wine and watching TV. My stammered attempts at apology were immediately overwhelmed by an eruption of warmth and joy. "Benvenuto! Welcome to our campground! I am so glad that you are here … oh, and there are children! Wonderful! Let me show you around, you can pick any spot you like …" Wine was offered, embraces were exchanged, and my children concluded based on sample size of two that Switzerland and Italy offered the world's starkest contrast in campground keepers.

It was a happy but road-weary Cogdell family that pulled into Herrnhut, Germany, for the Antioch Network gathering. Little did we know our lives were about to change.

It was in Herrnhut that George and Hanna Miley entered the story. Though we had never known the Mileys personally, our paths had crossed several times years before. We always thought of them in the context of their vision for church-planting in unreached countries. What we did not know is that the Spirit had since led George and Hanna on an unexpected journey as well.

Hanna was a Jew who escaped Germany in 1939 on the Kindertransport to England. Seeing the increasing persecution and imprisonment of Jews under the Nazi regime, Hanna's parents had made the excruciating decision to send their daughter out of her home country into the arms of strangers. Hanna's parents were eventually taken by train to Poland, where they were killed by the Nazis.

In 1999, Hanna heard God inviting her to return to Germany to research the birthplaces of her parents.[2] At the time, Hanna still felt great bitterness and anger toward the German people. She and George ended up in Gemünd, her childhood home, where townsfolk helped her begin to recover some of her lost memories. The Mileys returned the next year with a group of intercessors. As they prayed, God began to dissolve Hanna's hard heart and replace it with a love for German people. By 2008, they had committed to live in Gemünd half of each year working for reconciliation, forgiveness, and healing of the wounds of the past.[3]

When we arrived in Herrnhut, the Mileys made a point to greet us. George invited us to lead prayer at the first morning session. The request caught us by surprise as we considered ourselves visitors, outsiders. "Well, you do lead a house of prayer," they reminded us. We could not argue with that, so we agreed, thinking that would be the extent of our input. Once again, we were mistaken. The Mileys had another interest in our family.

After serving for decades as Protestant missionaries, George and Hanna had begun to explore the riches of liturgical prayer. They had been deeply moved

---

2 I find it interesting that this occurred in the same year that Amy was being drawn into the Catholic Church and that I was receiving the power plant of prayer vision.

3 See https://hannamiley.com/ for more of Hanna's story of reconciliation as a survivor of the Holocaust, and also the Afterword, which is written by Hanna.

by the writings of church fathers and Christian mystics. They had partnered with Catholics in prayer for the Eifel region surrounding Gemünd, and now they carried a burden for unity in the body of Christ. In fact, George had taken the unprecedented step of inviting a Catholic priest to speak at this year's Antioch Network gathering. So they wanted to hear the story of our Catholic–Protestant marriage. The group responded warmly as Amy recounted her experience of Christ's pain over the divisions in his body.

We were awed to have wandered into a missions gathering that also closely reflected our own sense of calling! These teachers carried our vision for unity in the Church, but with greater knowledge and maturity than we had. Clearly this trip had been orchestrated by our loving Father, who was giving us a gift beyond all we could have asked or imagined.

The meeting in Herrnhut. George Miley is on the far left and his wife, Hanna, is on the far right. Father Peter is to the left of the cross, in the white shirt. Our friend Sandi Pedrotti from Hope Chapel is in the front–she had known of Father Peter previously and came to Herrnhut in part to hear him speak. Photo by Thomas Cogdell.

One aspect of this gift was an introduction to Father Peter Hocken, the Catholic priest George had invited. Father Peter was a recognized expert on the Pentecostal movement of the twentieth century. He was also a champion of the emerging Messianic Jewish churches. Toward the end of the gathering, this erudite British scholar engaged in a dialogue with another speaker, Paul Miller of YWAM, about the necessity of Catholics and Protestants working together in evangelism. They spoke realistically, but with great faith, concerning the challenges of Catholic–Protestant unity. We knew we would never forget that talk between "Peter and Paul," but we never imagined Father Peter would take note of us.

Toward the end of our time there, Amy—who was still a bit shy around Catholic clergy—worked up her courage to ask Father Peter's blessing on the crosses and rosaries we had purchased in La Verna. For Catholics, a priest's blessing on such objects carries spiritual value. She did not want to bother the great man, but this was a unique opportunity. Father Peter dutifully complied, then carried on with his business. However, a short time later, Father Peter walked over to the table where we were eating. He began to prophesy about our ministry! We soaked it in, and were even more delighted at his last statement. "I think I will come visit you," he said, with a twinkle in his eye.

Many others whom we met in Herrnhut would continue to play significant roles in our lives. Julia Stone. David and Greetje Sanders. The Thurman family. Hans Wiedenmann. Our dear friend from Hope Chapel Sandi Pedrotti was also there. In the years that followed, she would become an increasingly important co-laborer in the work of Wittenberg 2017.

> "I think I will come visit you," he said, with a twinkle in his eye. ... Amy and I felt like hobbits at the council of Elrond in Rivendell.

And ... our children loved Herrnhut! This lovely little German town felt like both a safe haven and a world of freedom. Each morning we gave the children a few euros and told them when to be back for lunch. They would return hungry and happy, relating tales of adventure in the town and surrounding woods. A few more euros would exchange hands, and the gang of four would reinvade Herrnhut for the afternoon. They never asked us to make good on our promise to leave as soon as they were bored by the conference.

On the last day of the gathering, George and Hanna asked to meet with us privately. They expressed interest in becoming more closely connected, and even mentioned the possibility of holding an Antioch gathering in Austin.

Amy and I felt like hobbits at the council of Elrond in Rivendell. Our heads were spinning, not with dread but with the wonder of being drawn unexpectedly into a larger world. We were sad when the gathering concluded.

As we drove away from Herrnhut, Amy turned to me and spoke words that would prove prescient:

"If anyone could pull off the Wittenberg meeting, it would be these people."

 Use the QR code or visit **https://bit.ly/w17ch10** to explore a map, more pictures, and additional material for this chapter, including what happens when Cogdell boys find the world's biggest snowball in Hitler's secret hideout in the Austrian Alps.

Chapter 11

God Does It

I will never forget the time when our whole mixed group of Catholics, Protestants, Free Church people and Messianic Jews were praying in St. Peter's Cathedral in Rome. We stood, sat, or kneeled in a side aisle, off the tourist stream, identified with and confessed the sins of the very people responsible for the erection of this magnificent building centuries ago. They had their share in the unholy story of indulgences and the abuse of power that finally led to the Protestant Reformation and the split of the Church. I was deeply moved as I saw Catholics, including a bishop, kneeling beside me, weeping and crying to God. It is the grace of God that brings us together to the foot of the cross.

Franz Rathmair, Pentecostal with Anabaptist and Catholic roots, Austrian Round Table, Steyr, Austria

During one of many dinners at our table we had Messianic Jews, Catholics, Lutherans, and some nondenominational friends. The conversation got a little tense. I asked the Lord how can we be in unity when there is such dramatic difference in some of our beliefs? And I saw a picture of the encampment of Israel. Every tribe in its own tent. With their own traditions, values, treasures, and many mistakes. The presence in the middle of the camp brings righteousness, holiness, purpose, and correction. The kingdom is in tents. We just need to agree to wait and prepare for his return together. This changed how I see unity in the body.

Marianna Gol, Messianic Jew, founder and leader of Streams in the Desert, Beersheba, Israel

For anyone who doubts that God has a sense of humor …

We pulled our tiny rental car back into the Berlin airport, after our last European swing through Poland. (We loved Poland!) As we lugged our bags up to the check-in counter, we began praying over them—as we had done before leaving three weeks ago—that God would bring each of them safely through to the airport at the end. Then my wife prayed something uncharacteristically mischievous: "But, Lord, it's OK if they lose the broken tent."

And sure enough, back in Texas eleven bags instead of twelve appeared on the conveyor belt. The tent had been swallowed into the bowels of some baggage labyrinth. We were able to buy an entire replacement tent with the check sent to us by the apologetic airline. Amy has seen a lot of her prayers answered in miraculous ways through the years … but heaven must have been laughing at this one.

We readjusted to life after the Herrnhut trip. Our horizons were wider, but our bank account was smaller. I threw myself back into my Athens Group work and soon got a surprise. Our CEO took me to lunch at a local Mexican food dive.

"You are now an oil and gas consultant," he said to me over blue-corn chicken enchiladas. What?!

I was working at the time in the cushy corporate headquarters of Whole Foods Market. And now I was facing the prospect of work on offshore oil rigs—hardly known for their creature comforts.

But God was in this transition. In my new position, I began to travel. The Netherlands … Norway … even as far as Singapore. To my surprise, I discovered that I loved it!

On my first business trip to Norway, I discovered the most beautiful place in the world–Preikestolen (Pulpit Rock) above Lysefjord (the Light Fjord). Photo by Thomas Cogdell.

Just getting on a plane was enough to make my heart happy. Being able to take my Nikon camera to a new country made me giddy. And best of all, I was flying business class! I had always assumed that it was impossible to produce decent food for humans on an airplane. Suddenly, the curtain was pushed back (literally), and I was ushered into a world of stainless steel silverware, bubbling champagne, and four-course dinners served on fine china.

I had also assumed that frequent-flier programs were a scam. Who could earn even one free ticket? Now I discovered who could—business class customers like me! My miles piled up quickly. The problem changed from never having enough miles for a free ticket, to having so many miles that it was hard to imagine finding the time to get away.

God, of course, had a plan for all those miles.

I also rejoiced when a work assignment took me to Europe. My flights always went through Amsterdam. And Amsterdam was reasonably close to Gemünd, Germany—where George and Hanna Miley lived. Often my work schedule was flexible enough that I could take a few days off to rent a car and visit them. I loved photographing Hanna, meeting their German friends, and praying with them as they listened to the Lord's leading for their ministry of reconciliation.

While on a business trip to Germany for Athens Group, I took this picture of Hanna at the Holocaust Memorial in Berlin. In 2017, I submitted it to National Geographic on a whim, and they immediately published it on their YourShot website, where it garnered hundreds of votes for top photo of the day, and dozens of comments from viewers touched by Hanna's story. Photo by Thomas Cogdell.

Back at home, AHOP continued to grow. We had five wonderful young people on staff. While I was working at Athens Group or traveling across the world, they were coordinating unceasing prayer in local churches, conducting youth camps, and devoting much of their time to praying for reconciliation in the body of Christ. Surely God heard those prayers, rising like incense from a small room in a forgotten warehouse on the east side of Austin. How often heaven's purposes are set in motion by hidden acts of faithful, fervent prayer!

In the summer of 2009, George and Hanna came to Austin. Not just them, but the entire Antioch Network. We had dreamed of hosting a Herrnhut-like gathering at AHOP ... and now they were calling us from the airport, asking for directions. To have many of those whom we had met in Germany come to us? Well, it was simply wonderful. In particular, reconnecting with David and Greetje Sanders and Julia Stone from Berlin would soon prove to be important.

Amy had also followed up with Father Peter Hocken, and he visited AHOP in the spring of 2010. What a treasure Father Peter was! We sat at his feet and soaked in all he was saying, amazed that this well-known scholar and international speaker was taking an interest in our little community of prayer and reconciliation.

It was earlier in 2010 that I had received a seemingly run-of-the-mill email in my Athens Group office. There was an oil and gas assignment for me in southern Germany, probably in March. I paid little attention, assuming I would be notified when the date was fixed.

In late February, another email came. My work in Germany was postponed for a few months. They weren't ready for me yet. Delays like this are typical in the oil rig business.

In the summer, I received a third email. They were still not ready—look for communication in August. I filed it away and went back to my regular work.

In August: "Almost ready. We'll let you know for sure in September." Well, I wasn't going to hold my breath.

Then the email arrived in September. I can picture it as clearly today as if I were back there at my desk, staring at my computer screen, reading each word carefully.

I needed to be on the ground in Germany, ready to work, on … Monday, November 1, 2010.

I was immediately transported back to that pivotal moment on the Autobahn. My mind's eye was staring longingly at the fast-approaching exit ramp to Wittenberg.

"… Or, you can pass it by, and let me do it."

Two years later, God had done it.

Not only was I going to Germany, I could arrange my travel such that I could visit Wittenberg before starting my job.

Not only was I heading to Wittenberg, I was being flown business class, all-expenses-paid by a major oil company.

And now I had friends in Berlin, who could help me reserve a room for a prayer meeting in 2017—the prayer meeting I had first envisioned with Amy while flying home from our anniversary trip to Switzerland.

And then, Holy Spirit chills began to run up and down my spine.

God's math was not "a little fuzzy," as I had been willing to oh-so-generously grant him back in 2008. It was divine precision.

You see, my visit to Wittenberg would be on Sunday, October 31.

October 31 was Reformation Day.

And Reformation Day in 2010 was seven years—to the day—from the 500th anniversary in 2017.

So the words "seven years" that I had originally heard in 2000, and then discarded in 2007, were actually from God all along! I had just misinterpreted them. I had thought they represented seven years forward from 2000, when in fact the correct interpretation was seven years *backward* from 2017. How often we assume that our initial interpretation of God's words is the right one! How many "surprises of the Spirit" we are in for when we review our lives in heaven!

I read again the work email that was opening the way to Wittenberg.

And I knew beyond the shadow of a doubt that God had *something* planned for 2017.

Use the QR code or visit **https://bit.ly/w17ch11** to explore more pictures and additional material for this chapter, including pictures you might not want to see, of what you're missing airplane-food-wise if you're not traveling in first class.

Chapter 12

"Seven Years from Today"

It's wonderful and exciting to see the Holy Spirit leading men and women of God from America to Germany to serve us. We believe that God has connected America and Germany in a special way to bring fruit for his kingdom.

PETRA FEDDERSEN and BIRGIT JANKE, senior leaders of FCJG and HELP International, Lüdenscheid, Germany

In October 2017, my wife Tanya and I attended the ecumenical meeting in Wittenberg, Germany, with the permission of the patriarchal locum tenens at the time, Archbishop Karekin Bekçiyan, and the invitation of the Wittenberg 2017 initiative. It was one of the unique experiences in my life.

For five days Catholic, Lutheran, Baptist, Anabaptist, Anglican, Evangelical, Pentecostal, Messianic Jews were speaking, sharing presentations and prayers about interchurch peace with more than 400 participants from almost all denominations and many countries around the world. The only ones among those present who were from the Orthodox Church were me, Tanya, and one other young man. Everyone I met there showed deep respect and interest in the Orthodox Church and spirituality. This approach made me incredibly happy.

However, it was not the speeches that impressed me the most. There were different church representatives, a Catholic bishop, a Lutheran priest, a Pentecostal pastor, etc., who talked one by one and apologized for the mistakes their churches committed against other churches in history. In a world where hatred, exclusion, marginalization, judgment, disdain were so high and penetrated into every environment, people were humbly apologizing, forgiving each other, and hugging and crying. Brand-new and solid friendships were established.

I have been representing my church in ecumenical settings for more than twenty years. Wittenberg 2017 made me realize a fact that I know and experience, albeit partly, in a tangible and full feeling: interchurch unity is first of all apologizing with humility and forgiveness. The healing power of God was noticeably present in Wittenberg.

ARCHPRIEST DRTAD UZUNYAN, ecumenical representative of the Armenian Patriarchate of Turkey (Eastern Orthodox), Istanbul, Turkey

If I had taken the exit in 2008, I would have been alone in Wittenberg. Well, except for my upset family.

Julia took this picture of me in the Berlin train station, waiting for our train to Wittenberg. I had waited ten years; now I just had to wait another ten minutes! Photo by Julia Stone. Used with permission.

But in 2010, when I stepped off the train onto the Wittenberg railway platform, I was not alone. Julia Stone was with me.

Julia lived in Berlin. She was a British journalist with a typically lovely accent, at least to my Texan ears. She spoke German as well. What a gift to have Julia with me!

We had gotten to know Julia better since Herrnhut. I had come to trust her determination, her prophetic sensings, and her careful attention to detail. I had also come to appreciate her dry sense of humor. We inquired with a lady at the tourist information booth at the train station about meeting rooms in the city, and after her dismissive response Julia turned to me and remarked, "Well, *she* doesn't want us to be here." Not the most encouraging start.

But we struck gold across from the Schlosskirche in town. Schlosskirche means "Castle Church," and this was the famous church with the door—the Wittenberg door, to which Luther supposedly nailed the Ninety-Five Theses back in 1517.[1] They were smart to put the main tourist information center just across the cobbled street. Every American tourist wants to know where to find "The Door!"

Probably very few show an interest in "The Meeting Rooms" …

"Wait here a minute," the clerk said, and disappeared. When she reappeared, she produced a treasure map—a list of every meeting room available to rent in Wittenberg. Each entry showed the maximum number of people, the address, the website, the contact person … God bless the German attention to detail!

---

1 More about that myth in chapter 17.

We huddled over the list, pen in hand. Only five rooms could hold more than one hundred people. We circled them, noted the addresses, and determined to try to visit each one.

We also wanted to visit each of the three gates of the old city. Wittenberg was a typical—which means typically beautiful—German town. Some of the old city walls remained. And it was known where the gates of the medieval city were, through which Martin Luther would have passed in his day. We felt that it could be significant to pray at each of these spots.

Five meeting rooms. Three gates. And one more assignment.

Before leaving for Germany, I had asked for prayer at Hope Chapel. The person who prayed for me had told me to "look for John 17 in Wittenberg—this will be an important sign to you."[2] John 17, of course, recorded Jesus's pivotal prayer for his people—that we would be one. But how to look for it? All I could imagine was a stained glass window with a quotation on it.

So as we made our way through the old city of Wittenberg, praying at each gate and seeking out each meeting room, I determined to "keep a sharp eye peeled" for John 17.[3]

We came to the Stadtkirche—the City Church. I was already being educated in the layout and history of Wittenberg. The City Church was more important to the Reformation than the Castle Church, in spite of the Schlosskirche's famous door. It was the Stadtkirche where Luther set up his pastorate, after he was excommunicated from the Catholic Church. In other words, the City Church was the *first* Protestant church. "Mother Church of the Reformation," a placard proudly reads on the outside the church. We went inside and began looking around.

We first explored a small chamber in the back of the church. Perfect for prayer! We prayed together. Then Julia went up toward the altar, and I wandered around the other side of the church.

Toward the pulpit.

At the very spot where Martin Luther had preached.

---

2 These words came from John Bibee, a much beloved member of Hope Chapel. Until he died in 2018, he would stand at the front after each service, patiently listening to and praying with every person who came up to him.

3 A strangely vivid mixed metaphor that has somehow become common in our family.

The stairs leading to the elevated pulpit were … open? I looked again, more carefully. By this time, I had toured enough old churches in Europe to know that there was a variety of means to say the same thing: "None shall pass." A gate … a rope … a sign … there was always something barring the way. But on this pulpit, arguably the most historic and important of all I had seen so far—nothing. It was wide open.

To be honest, I knew I probably shouldn't ascend the pulpit steps in the heart of the Stadtkirche of Wittenberg. But I also knew that there would be a Bible in the pulpit. And part of me wondered … "Could it be open to John 17?" This would be a wonderful sign of favor from God!

And I figured I could always plead "being an American" in my defense.[4]

So I nervously climbed the stairs, expecting at any minute to be stopped by a strong German command. None came. I reached the top. I looked at the open Bible.

It was blank. Blank? How can a Bible be blank? Was it … a fake Bible??

The blank Bible in Luther's pulpit.
Photo by Thomas Cogdell.

I drew nearer to investigate. Upon closer inspection, I saw that the Bible in the pulpit was open to the intertestamental pages—the pages between the Old and the New Testaments.

I was disappointed. While hoping against hope that the Bible would be open to John 17, I kept in reserve the thought that it would be open to some scripture, at least, that might be construed to relate to our purpose. But … blankness.[5]

I turned around and sadly retraced my steps down. When I reached the bottom, I stopped suddenly. A thought came into my head. A wonderful, terrible, awful, and bold thought—"I can change that."

---

4 Among some Europeans (and in most other areas of the world as well), Americans have a reputation for being insensitive, disrespectful, and sometimes just plain stupid. Unfortunately, this reputation is mostly well deserved. I try to be a different kind of American, by learning the culture and respecting rules and norms—even those I don't understand. But occasionally I find it beneficial to be a little oblivious.

5 Wiser heads than mine would later interpret the very significant meaning of this blank page. See chapter 16.

There was no question that touching that Bible would be strictly "Verboten." This didn't stop me from going back up. I just went with more caution than before. I inched toward the front of the pulpit. I was now in plain view. Nobody paid me the least attention.

Turning over a "new page" in Luther's pulpit. Photo by Thomas Cogdell.

I began to turn the large, heavy pages.

The Bible was, of course, in German, but I knew the landscape of the Bible well enough to navigate in a foreign language. I came to the Gospel of John. I kept turning … John 10 … John 16 … and somehow it seemed just right that when I turned over the next page, John 17 began right at the top. It was, literally, the start of a new page.

The profound meaning of this action was immediately impressed upon me. Turning over a new page in Luther's home church. Changing from a page of division to a page of unity. Even in my astonishment, I thought to pull out my phone and take a picture of the Bible now newly opened to John 17.

> The profound meaning of this action was immediately impressed upon me. Turning over a new page in Luther's home church. Changing from a page of division to a page of unity.

When I went back down, Julia stood at the bottom of the stairs. She looked at me somewhat sharply, as if to say, "And what have you been up to?" I excitedly explained, and her prophetic sensibilities overrode her sense of propriety.

"You have to go see for yourself, Julia!" And the pulpit now had two trangressors.

After she came down, I decided to go back up with my phone and shoot a quick video of the church from the pulpit. I had become oblivious to the environment of a historical monument around me, lost in my giddiness of God's granting us the ability to find John 17 in the most unlikely yet most powerful of places.

This was one time too many. Here came the strong German voice, the one I had expected at the beginning—"*Halt!*" I returned to ground level and was called to account for my actions. I pleaded guilty innocence. "Why couldn't I go up? There was nothing telling me not to?" The resulting glare from the guard wilted me into silence. She produced a rope and fastened it across the stairs.

Julia and I left the Stadtkirche a little chastened ... but once outside we burst out into an astonished recounting of what had just happened. We both felt that it was a prophetic marker. We bowed our heads and thanked the Holy Spirit for giving us this wondrous surprise.

Then, we set ourselves to the impossible task of reserving a room.

The first room we tried was the Leucorea—odd to have a Greek name in this place, I thought. We passed through a narrow stone gate that opened in typical European fashion into a large inner courtyard. In Europe, it often seems that the inside is bigger than the outside. You have to penetrate the rather ordinary facade to find that what it masks is bigger and better than you expected. Very different than in America, where the facade is often impressive but the reality less so.

The doors were locked. We prayed. A group came out of the doors, so we slipped in before they clicked shut.

We wandered the halls until we came to the meeting room. Again, the doors were locked. Again, we prayed. Suddenly a woman rounded the corner with keys in her hand, opened the meeting room, and went inside. Julia and I glanced at each other with knowing looks, and followed her. We were clearly in God's hands.

It turned out this woman was the director of the Leucorea. She had popped in on this Saturday morning to check that the meeting room was ready for tomorrow's Reformation Day speeches. This was the nicest meeting room in Wittenberg, and intuitively I knew that we couldn't broach the subject of renting it for the 500th anniversary. Surely this is where the Lutheran Church royalty would be.

But we got her card, and she told us a little of the history of the building. This had been the University of Wittenberg, where the young Augustinian monk Martin Luther was a professor. He possibly lived and certainly taught in this building. Perhaps he even wrote some of the Ninety-Five Theses right here! In the intervening centuries, it had become quarters for the Prussian army, then an apartment block during the Soviet occupation of East Germany. In the 1990s, the American ambassador to Germany was looking for a place to have meetings in between Berlin and Frankfurt. He was a Lutheran, and his eyes lit upon Wittenberg. He arranged for the funds to restore the building and turn it into a world-class conference facility. "So we are very friendly to Americans here … my husband even has a library of American studies upstairs. Would you like to see it?"

The nicest facility in Wittenberg was friendly to Americans? What were the chances of that? Julia and I left wondering what the Lord's plans for this building were in 2017.

The next stop was a meeting room owned by the Lutheran Church. Our random arrival time seemed once again carefully orchestrated, because we showed up just as a group was leaving. We inquired about the room, and the leader of the group took us back inside to look at it. "You came at just the right time," he said. "Normally the room would be closed up on the Saturday before Reformation Day."

Julia in the Leucorea.
Photo by Thomas Cogdell.

In the end, we were able to see all five of the meeting rooms that we had circled at the beginning of the day. The Leucorea was one. Two others were too closely tied to the city or the Lutheran Church for us to even consider inquiring about a reservation in 2017—they would certainly be otherwise occupied. The fourth room was a large meeting hall that could hold 300, but its "German beer hall" ambience seemed incompatible with our purpose of prayer.

The last room that Julia and I visited together was in the Best Western hotel. I was surprised to find that this was one of the nicest hotels in Wittenberg. In the United States, Best Western is more of a budget brand. But here was a lovely lobby, crystal chandeliers, and dark wood paneling. We asked at the desk if we could see the meeting room. A very nice young woman led us down the hall and unlocked the door to the Melanchtonsaal—the room named after Philip Melanchton, Luther's compatriot in the Reformation. It was actually a suite of three rooms—a lobby, a smaller room, and a larger room that could hold 100 people. Altogether, a group of 150 would easily be able to come and go. I could immediately imagine a prayer meeting in this room.

I checked in discreetly with Julia to see what she thought. "Yes, looks good to me," she said. We both agreed that a hotel was "neutral territory," much likelier to suit our purposes than any of the other four rooms. We trooped back up to the front desk.

"Would you like to reserve the room?" our host asked.

"Yes," I replied. "I am an American businessman, and I'm interested in reserving your meeting room." I handed her my Athens Group business card—the only one I had.

She looked at the card. "And when would you like the room, Herr Cogdell?"

I took a deep breath. "Seven years from today."

Her eyes widened. But her professionalism overcame her curiosity. "I can do this for you. But I must tell you, so far in advance I cannot give you a firm price."

"Kein problem." (No problem.)

As she pulled out the reservation book for 2017, I was again thankful for the ability of the German people to maintain a structured order in their lives and businesses. A reservation seven years in advance would have no meaning in a country like Mexico, Turkey, or China. But I had confidence that in Germany, if the reservation was written down, it would be honored.

The rest of the time at the desk, I tried to remain outwardly calm while inwardly my spirit was dancing. As Julia and I walked back to the train station, we rejoiced together in the events of the day. It seemed that God had orchestrated each step, so that we always arrived at the right place, at the right time.

We now had a reservation for a prayer meeting in 2017—amazing!

What should we do with it? I had no clue …

As my children grew up, I was always amused at the many early graduation ceremonies. "Why do they even have a *kindergarten* graduation, Amy?" But I have come to see the wisdom of celebrating small but significant steps toward a larger goal.

The fulfillment of the number "7" spoken in 2000 with the reservation of a room in Wittenberg, exactly seven years before the 500th anniversary, was like this. A graduation ceremony. Back in the heady "born again, again" days, the Holy Spirit had enrolled Amy and me in the "voice of God" school. And we had learned to hear him directly—through dreams, visions, and inner sensings of God speaking.

The reservation was a "well done!" from God, a kindergarten graduation diploma. And we had now matriculated into the next class in the same school.

Could we learn to hear the voice of God … through other people?

Use the QR code or visit **https://bit.ly/w17ch12** to explore more pictures and additional material for this chapter, including what happened on the actual Reformation Day in Wittenberg (the stories from this chapter took place on Saturday, November 30, the day before the 493rd anniversary).

Midword

By John Dawson

At this point, Wittenberg 2017 moves from a personal story to the story of a team. I described my experience of personal repentance for my compulsions in chapter 8. We are all familiar with personal repentance. But what does corporate repentance look like? Is it even a biblical concept? John Dawson draws from his decades of experience leading corporate identificational repentance to help us understand the answers to these important questions.

—Thomas Cogdell

First Peter teaches us that there is an important purpose for our unity. Believers are like living stones being built together as a spiritual house (1 Pet 2:5). The purpose of this structure is to offer up spiritual sacrifices acceptable to a holy creator. The writer then goes on to liken the redeemed in Christ, both Jew and non-Jew, to the Jewish priesthood.

What did he mean by this? What did the priests do that models for us something of our responsibility today? Essentially the priests were intercessors. They made atonement for the land. They stood in the gap between God and human beings and mediated on behalf of the people a needed atonement for sin. They presented sacrifices for both the sin of the nation and the sin of individuals.

"Isn't that all in the past?" some might ask. "Didn't the Reformers point out that the priesthood of all believers under the new covenant negates any need for a human priesthood?" The answer: yes. The Reformers *did* protest the *exclusive* prerogative of a religious hierarchy, but they were not against prayer. They called for every believer to approach God personally, experience salvation through faith in Christ alone, and then walk with God in daily conversation that included interceding for others. Calvin, Zwingli, Luther, and Knox were men of prayer who cried out to God for spiritual breakthrough in their generation just like Ezra, Nehemiah, Jeremiah, Daniel, and the other great reformers described in the Scriptures.

The essential difference between us as New Testament priests and the Old Testament priesthood is that the ancient priests looked *forward* by faith to the atonement Messiah would provide while we look *backward* 2,000 years to the same hinge point of history. They presented the blood of animals, a *physical* sacrifice, in contrast to the priesthood 1 Peter describes, which offers up a *spiritual* sacrifice—making claim by faith on the shed blood of Jesus as the final atonement for sin.

It is important to realize that priestly mediation is part of the ongoing ministry of Jesus. He is our great "high priest" who "ever lives to make intercession for us."[1] The fact that a perfect sacrifice was made for our sin over 2,000 years ago does not automatically resolve all our problems, but rather secures the grounds for all reconciliation. The ministry of reconciliation is ongoing. Or to put it another way: the blood has been made available; however, the blood must still be applied. We must make a conscious choice to believe in the power of Christ's atonement, receive his indwelling presence, and turn from sin.

Interceding for our nation, city, or people group involves a deliberate choice to face the reality of sin—to uncover it, grieve over it, acknowledge the damage it has done, and then appropriate the delivering grace of God by faith. Satan always attempts to keep hidden the defilement of the land through historic sins. Furthermore, the enemy struggles to keep the Church from its priestly role of asking for forgiveness and leading the way in repentance. This is why Paul exhorts, "first of all, that requests, prayers, intercession and thanksgiving be made for everyone" (1 Tim 2:1). The majority of a population may be continuing in their sin; however, a righteous remnant interceding on their behalf can bring down mercy on the undeserving. We must never underestimate the power that is released when united believers intercede in humility. The Old Testament restoration books—Ezra, Nehemiah, Jeremiah, and Daniel—demonstrate how a believing remnant can set in motion the healing of even a divided, shattered, dispossessed nation. Most important was the heart attitude of these intercessors as they prayed the prayer of identification (emphasis added).

> Because of *our sins and the iniquities of our fathers*, Jerusalem and Thy people have become a reproach to all around us. (Dan 9:16, NJKV)
>
> I am praying before Thee now, day and night, on behalf of the sons of Israel Thy servants, confessing the sins of the sons of Israel which we have sinned against Thee; *I and my father's house have sinned.* (Neh 1:6)

---

1 All scripture quotes in the midword are from John Dawson's teaching notes.

O my God, I am ashamed and embarrassed to lift up my face to Thee, my God, for our iniquities have risen above our heads … Since the days of our fathers to this day we have been in great guilt. (Ezra 9:6–7)

Humility and genuine brokenness released God's favor for he "opposes the proud, but gives grace to the humble" (James 4:6). The Lord taught Israel how to seek this favor by instructing her high priest to enter the Holy of Holies once a year on the Day of Atonement. In a posture of great humility, he identified with the sin of the people. This model was fulfilled and made perfect in the Person of Jesus, but the spirit of intercession still seeks those who will stand before God in prayer on behalf of those who either cannot, do not know how to, or will not pray for themselves. Jesus has now called every believer into his own ministry—the ministry of reconciliation (2 Cor 5:18–21).

The Wounds of the World

When we study human conflict, we see that Satan's method of getting one group to abuse another is rooted in the hardheaded collision of self-righteous people within each group. Take *some* truth, polarize the people with different *sides* of that truth, tempt them to unrighteous judgment, then watch them wound one another with rejection, harsh words, and injustice. The cycle seems endless, since even as two individuals can hurt each other through selfish and unjust behavior, it is equally common for wounds to be sustained by a nation or people within a nation. Animosities and bitterness can fester unresolved for generations.

> Take *some* truth, polarize the people with different *sides* of that truth, tempt them to unrighteous judgment, then watch them wound one another with rejection, harsh words, and injustice.

How do we respond to such deep, gaping, sometimes ancient wounds? The answer lies in the humility of Jesus expressed through his body, the Church.

A Model for Reconciliation

The ministry of reconciliation is the responsibility of the living Church. There is no substitute for the atonement Jesus provided for sin. Deep repentance, leading to personal and societal change, has gone hand in hand with past revivals. If we as Christians are to respond meaningfully to the tensions and injustices of our day, we must model and initiate repentance. The biblical pattern for spiritual recovery involves four actions: confession, repentance, reconciliation, and restitution.

- *Confession:* Stating the truth; acknowledging the unjust or hurtful actions of myself or my people group toward other people or categories of people.
- *Repentance:* Turning from unloving to loving actions.
- *Reconciliation:* Expressing and receiving forgiveness and pursuing intimate fellowship with previous enemies.
- *Restitution:* Attempting to restore that which has been damaged or destroyed and seeking justice wherever we have power to act or to influence those in authority to act.

Sometimes we can begin this process by organizing events or ceremonies in which representatives of offending and offended subcultures have an opportunity to express regret and extend forgiveness. Wittenberg 2017 was a series of such gatherings.

In initiating these events, we recognize that the issues involved are complex. We must accept the task of honoring the righteous deeds of our ancestors while acknowledging their sins. Truth dictates that we embrace both the guilt and the grandeur that has attached itself to our various cultural, ethnic, or national identities. In such representative intercession, this fundamental point of understanding is essential: though each person stands alone before God and is in *no way* guilty for the sins of his or her ancestors or any other group, a willing intercessor *may* volunteer to open herself before God, to experience godly sorrow, and to confess the sins of the people or the land with which she identifies. This is where reconciliation begins.

The Example of Jesus

Jesus concerned himself with corporate entities as well as persons. He ministered to his people group as a nation with a particular history. He wept over Israel's sins and wounds. He identified with them. He was absolutely rooted in their story for it was his story, as the genealogy in Matthew 1 reveals.

The most striking example of Jesus dealing with a corporate entity among his people is found in Matthew 23:29–32. Notice:

> "Woe to you, scribes and Pharisees, hypocrites! For you build the tombs of the prophets and adorn the monuments of the righteous, and say: 'If we had lived in the days of our fathers, we would not have been partners with them in shedding the blood of the prophets.' Consequently you bear witness against yourselves, that you are the sons of those who murder the prophets. Fill up then the measure of the guilt of your fathers."

Here, Jesus ascribes unresolved corporate guilt to a multigenerational, vocational cast—the scribes and Pharisees. Jesus indicates that the proof of their unresolved guilt was that they took a position of self-righteous accusation toward their forefathers rather than humbly identifying with them. Because of this, all opportunity for cleansing was lost and the weight of unresolved sin rested upon their shoulders.

> Stephen totally identifies with his people, even as some of their number engaged in the act of killing him.

In contrast to this scripture, compare the righteous example of identificational repentance in the testimony of Stephen (Acts 7). Even more radically than the great intercessory examples of Ezra, Nehemiah, Jeremiah, and Daniel, Stephen totally identifies with his people, even as some of their number engaged in the act of killing him. He doesn't say "You Jews," but rather, "*our* fathers were unwilling to be obedient to him," constant in this spirit of humility until, falling on his knees as stones rain upon him, he cries out, "Lord, *do not hold this against them*" (Acts 7:60; emphasis added). Truly this is the power of the cross at work in the early Church. The first Christians show us the way.

What was effective then is just as important in today's missionary endeavors. Intercession is more than prayer; it is living out the mediating, reconciling life of Christ in a wounded, bitter world with no answers for broken relationships. This is a day of God's favor, a fulfillment of that which was prophesied long ago: "you will be called the priests of the Lord; you will be spoken of as ministers of our God" (Isa 61:6).

Part III

A Journey into Repentance,
2010–2015

Chapter 13

"Where Are the Jews?"

One vivid memory is being surrounded by the jubilant Austrian children as they led us in Hebrew song and dance. The John 17 impact of our unity, or lack thereof, directly affects our children and the future generations of our planet. Being led by the children was like being invited by Jesus himself into the perichoresis / love-dance of the Holy Trinity and the JOY of living out our crucial and urgent role as ambassadors of reconciliation.

Another memory was the beauty and wonder of being exposed to Messianic Judaism, and how that opens an entirely different lens into Christian unity. By better understanding the first wounding of unity when the nascent Christian community not only eschewed its Jewish roots, but aggressively persecuted the Jewish people, scapegoating them with the charge of deicide, one sees how we have become tragically separated from our "elder brothers and sisters" in the faith, and how Christian praxis became horrifically complicit in sowing the anti-Semitic seeds that led to the Shoah / Holocaust. Meeting thoughtful, serious Messianic Jews was a beautiful manifestation of the Pentecostal spirit of healing unity in our times.

NATE and JENNY BACON, Roman Catholic, regional directors for
InnerChange, Quetzaltenango, Guatemala

Thank you for initiating Wittenberg 2017 and for including the Messianic Jews in it.s

HANS WIEDENMANN, counselor and therapist,
Evangelical Lutheran Church, Germany

It's funny how you can look forward to something for a long time, yet not know what to do when it actually arrives. So it was with the room in Wittenberg.

For ten years my thoughts had been bent toward renting a room for a prayer meeting in 2017, on the 500th anniversary of the Protestant Reformation. Now ... I had the room!

So … what next? I honestly didn't know.

After I left Wittenberg with a room reserved for 2017, I traveled to southern Germany for my Athens Group work. I wrapped that up on Friday and my Monday morning flight was out of Berlin. Providentially, George and Hanna Miley were in Berlin that same weekend. So we arranged to spend Saturday afternoon together. We took advantage of the lovely hospitality of David and Greetje Sanders. We had met them at the oh-so-crucial 2008 Antioch Network meeting in Herrnhut. David is British, and Greetje is Dutch. They live in an apartment just a few blocks from the Hauptbahnhof, the iconic main train station in Berlin, which made it easy for Julia Stone and her roommate, Cynthia, to jump on the S-bahn train near their home and join us, as well.

The late afternoon sun slanted through the windows as Julia and I recounted the story of the previous weekend's trip to Wittenberg. The Mileys listened carefully—until Greetje distracted us all with the 4:00 PM German custom of *Kaffee und Kuchen*, coffee and sweets!

As we balanced our plates on our laps, I turned to George and surprised myself by saying, "I would like Wittenberg 2017 to be an initiative of Antioch Network."

I can still hear George's response in my mind. "Thomas, for you to say that really honors us. If Wittenberg 2017 happens, it cannot be an Austin thing. It cannot be a Texas thing. It cannot be an American thing. It must be owned by German Lutherans."

We settled on the following plan. I would come to Europe as often as I could—and with Amy, when possible. George and Hanna would then try to arrange meetings with the German Lutheran pastors they knew.

George left me with a somber warning.

Germans, he said, don't take quickly to new ideas.

Especially new ideas coming from an American.

And new ideas coming from an American involving an event as close to the German national psyche as Martin Luther's Reformation? Well … "Don't get your hopes up, Thomas."

Our meeting with Hans and Claudia Wiedenmann, facilitated by the Mileys, took place on the balcony of the Kurparkhotel in Gemünd, Germany—where hotelier Detlef Wurst welcomes many of the Miley's friends. Photo by Thomas Cogdell.

"Remember, don't get your hopes up." George looked at me and Amy lovingly as he repeated his words from the previous November. The date was April 23, 2011. The two small rivers that met in Gemünd were in their springtime glory, rushing toward each other with snowmelt-filled abandon, and joining forces to cascade onward through a tunnel of flowering trees. We were in the Kurparkhotel, a small inn owned by one of George and Hanna's friends. An outdoor table on a small upstairs patio was ready to receive the first German Lutheran leader to hear the vision of Wittenberg 2017.

Hans Wiedenmann had a friendly but reserved manner. His beautiful wife, Claudia, comported herself with great dignity. They extended their hands to me in a warm greeting. I was just nervous.

Over the course of the afternoon, we told them the story recounted in the first half of this book. They listened intently. George and Hanna helped when translation was necessary. Then there was quiet.

As Hans opened his mouth to respond, I braced myself for disappointment.

He said three things.

First—this idea is from God. *(Whew! I can relax a little now …)*

Second—this vision had to come through an American, because no German would have thought of approaching the 500th anniversary in this manner. *(No wonder God brought a Texan to Germany!)*

Third—"Where are the Jews?" *(Wait … what? The Jews?!)*

I had been relieved at his first response, and amused at his second. But the third bewildered me. He might as well have said, "Where are the little green men from Mars?" It would have as much relevance, in my mind, to the topic of Catholic–Protestant reconciliation.

But I was willing to set my confusion aside. A German Lutheran was on board with the basic vision! This was much more than we expected from this first meeting. George showed his somewhat surprised pleasure after the Wiedenmanns had said their goodbyes and returned to their home on the other side of the River Rhine.

The next German Lutheran was also named Hans. Hans Scholz pastored a Lutheran congregation in Bavaria, a region more heavily populated with Catholics than the rest of Germany. George and Hanna had mentioned Hans and his wife Rita to us many times. They had tried and failed to set up several meetings. The Scholzes kept a busy schedule!

The date of our meeting, 11/11/11, was numerically curious, but I found the location of the meeting more intriguing: a Catholic shrine called Schoenstatt.[1]

So when Hans and Rita sat down with me, my first question was of course: "What is a German Lutheran pastor doing in a Catholic shrine, anyway?" It turns out Hans wasn't the only Lutheran pastor on the premises. There was an entire convocation of them! They had booked facilities in Schoenstatt for a conference, not thinking twice about the fact that it was a Catholic location. For them, it was simply a beautiful place to have a meeting.

---

1 A shrine is a building considered holy or special, usually because of its association with a saint. I had already learned that Catholics really treasure shrines, in the same way perhaps that a typical Protestant might treasure a favorite Bible.

In a further twist, they had invited a Roman Catholic as their keynote speaker—Dr. Johannes Hartl, who had started the Augsburg Gebetshaus—a house of prayer similar to AHOP. So ... a German Roman Catholic theologian carrying a Protestant American house of prayer vision ... was addressing Lutheran pastors ... at a Catholic shrine. My head was spinning.

As I launched into the Wittenberg 2017 story, I wondered what Hans and Rita were thinking. I ended the same way I had with the Wiedenmanns: "So we have a room reserved ... what should we do with it?"

Praying with Hans, Rita, and George in the Schoenstatt dining room. Photo by Thomas Cogdell.

I quickly learned that Hans Scholz was as intense as Hans Wiedenmann was gentle. He and Rita were people of action. Hans stood up and paced back and forth. Then he stopped suddenly and turned to me.

"This idea is from God. A German would have never thought of this. But ... where are the Jews?"

If I was bewildered the first time around, the second time I was dumbfounded. What were the chances that the first two German Lutheran reactions would be, almost word for word, the same? I knew immediately I had to take this question about the Jews seriously, even if I didn't understand it.

I asked Hans why he asked about Jewish participation.

"We are in Germany, Thomas. The Jews are the key to everything. If we don't have Messianic Jews at this meeting, we won't have the favor of God upon us." Messianic Jews? "Where are the Jews?" had become ... where are the Messianic Jews? My mind's eye traveled back in time to the previous spring.

In May 2011, Amy and I found ourselves in Hainburg, about as far east as you can go in Austria. Hainburg was the home of Father Peter Hocken. On Father Peter's first visit to Austin, he had invited Amy and I to join a prayer group that met annually in Hainburg. This was an invitation we couldn't turn down!

At a break in that prayer meeting, Father Peter pulled me aside. He told me that he was going to give me ten minutes to share the vision of Wittenberg 2017. I was immediately apprehensive. I had to condense into ten minutes the story that usually took me two hours (or twelve chapters!) to tell fully. Amy warned me sternly that it would *not* be good to go over the allotted time.

Among those listening around the circle of chairs were Scots, Brits, Germans, Poles, and an Australian who helped organize the 2000 Olympics in Sydney. A single New Yorker sufficed to balance out three Texans. A nuclear physicist from France was writing in real time a translation of everything that was said, for the benefit of the mostly deaf woman from Belgium who sat next to him, eyes intent on the neat handwritten French unfolding the conversation around them. And over all of them, Father Peter presided with good humor and sharp questions.

Once again ... what were we Cogdells doing here?

And what would Father Peter think about Wittenberg 2017? How would he respond?

I felt the Holy Spirit give me a path through the story that would be relevant for this group, and (whew!) I finished just before my ten minutes were up.

> I was also surprised at the first person to raise her hand. It was Marianna Gol.

Father Peter cleared his throat and spoke up in his lovely British way. "Anyone from the group who feels moved to join this initiative, please raise your hand." I looked up, surprised at this generosity. I was also surprised at the first person to raise her hand. It was Marianna Gol.

Marianna is a joy. Marianna is fun, expressive, bold, and prophetic. Marianna is a superb cook. And Marianna is a Messianic Jew.

This memory from Hainburg now flooded into my mind in Schoenstatt, and suddenly the pieces began to fit together. I turned to Hans Scholz. "Actually, we do have a Messianic Jew involved."

"Good," his low voice rumbled over me in a wonderfully satisfied way.

When I later discussed this conversation with George and Hanna, they looked at me in a bemused fashion. "Thomas, Hanna is a Jew who believes that Jesus is the Jewish messiah. That makes her a Messianic Jew," George gently reminded me. Hanna added, "Also, Julia Stone has Jewish roots in her family tree. Though I don't know that she would call herself a 'Messianic Jew,' at least not yet ..."

Where were the Jews? God had already introduced us to some of them.— Marianna Gol, Hanna Miley, Julia Stone—I am so grateful. Marianna, Hanna, and Julia were each to play a pivotal role in Wittenberg 2017. And there were other Messianic Jews that we were yet to meet.

Surely it was God who moved both German Lutheran leaders of the same name to ask the same question. Which meant this was God's first question to the Wittenberg 2017 team. Why did it concern ... Messianic Jews?

All of God's questions are deep and complex. Some answers to this one became clear in the ensuing years.[2] But it may be helpful here to expound more generally on the unique role of Messianic Jews in Christian reconciliation. It can be summarized with a statement George Miley has often made:

> "When the Messianic Jew walks into the room, everything changes."

The first question is—what is meant by the term "Messianic Jew"?

We've already seen three different examples in this chapter.[3]

- Marianna Gol is a Jew who lives in Israel and does not belong to any other Christian tradition, but instead seeks both to follow Yeshua and to retain her Jewish identity as distinct from the Gentile Christian church.

- Hanna Miley is a Jew who lives in the United States and Germany, attends Anglican worship services with her husband George (who is an Anglican priest), and follows Jesus but does not, for example, try to keep Jewish traditions such as the feasts.

- Julia Stone was (at that time) a member of an independent, nondenominational church who was just discovering her Jewish ancestry and exploring what it might mean.

---

2 We were later to learn about Luther's anti-Semitism, and the subsequent use by Hitler of Luther's writings to justify Nazi atrocities.

3 Another category sometimes encountered is a Christian Gentile who discovers the Jewishness of their faith, and in their enthusiasm adopts Jewish ways—such as keeping Jewish holidays, praying with a prayer shawl, blowing a shofar, and so forth. For the purposes of this discourse, I would not consider this non-Jewish person to be a Messianic Jew.

For the examples of Marianna, Hanna, and Julia, there would be debate even among the Messianic Jews as to which of them might "qualify" for that name. From my outside "Gentile" perspective, I happily use the term Messianic Jew for all of them.

However, I also recognize that there is a special place for Jews like Marianna. These Messianic Jews do not belong to any Christian ecclesial community. They believe that Jesus is the Jewish Messiah, and—crucially—they seek to retain their Jewish identity. The reemergence of Messianic Jews such as these is one of the major "surprises of the Holy Spirit" of recent times, according to Father Peter. There simply have not been many followers of Jesus who visibly fit this pattern in a long, long time.[4] If the Church is pictured as a river with different currents and streams,[5] then the Messianic Jews are a stream that went underground after the first few centuries of the Church, but now has suddenly—surprisingly—surfaced again!

I have come to believe that Messianic Jews must play a pivotal role—perhaps *the* pivotal role—in reconciliation in the body of Christ. Why is this?

One reason is that the same description used above for today's Messianic Jews would apply to all of the first leaders of the Church in the New Testament. Peter, James, and John were not "Roman Catholic" or "Eastern Orthodox," and they were most certainly not "Protestant." They were faithful Jews who retained their Jewish identity, culture, and practices while also believing that Yeshua—their leader, friend, and fellow Jew—was the long-awaited Messiah. This means that all the other ecclesial communities of the Church trace their root and origin back to Messianic Jews. Which gives Messianic Jews a special place at the table.

Imagine a family where the older brother has been off in a distant land for years. The younger siblings have been reduced to continual squabbling. Suddenly the door opens and in walks the older brother. Immediately, this changes the dynamics between the younger siblings, providing them the opportunity to see their quarreling in a new light, and from a different

---

4 There have been many Jews who have been in the Church—converts to Catholicism, for example. But in order to take this step, they have surrendered their identity and culture as Jews to some degree—or often totally. But these should not be overlooked either. There is a new movement called Yachad BeYeshua to gather Jews who are in the churches and recognize their important contribution—see https://www.yachad-beyeshua.org for more details.

5 This metaphor is drawn from Revelation 19:6, and Richard Foster uses it wonderfully in his seminal book *Streams of Living Water*.

perspective. A very important question in our day, one that few are talking about, is how the Roman Catholic and Orthodox churches will respond to the emergence of the Messianic Jewish movement. For example, the presence of the "older brother" may challenge their current understanding of apostolic succession. I have heard a firsthand story of a well-known Roman Catholic leader who, upon meeting some Messianic Jews in the Vatican, said this: "If you are who you say you are, this is a major eschatological sign."

A second reason to consider carefully the role of Messianic Jews is that the majority of New Testament passages about reconciliation directly address hostility between Jews and Gentiles. If you've read this far, you may be familiar with passages about unity in Romans 14 and 15, Acts 15, and throughout Ephesians. The unity described is between … Jews and Gentiles! For example, Ephesians 2:14-21 describes Jesus making *these* two factions one by removing the dividing wall through the cross. Of course, all of these important biblical passages are not restricted to *only* Jew–Gentile hostility.[6] Without a doubt, principles of reconciliation can be discerned in these passages and applied to other divisions in the body of Christ. But they are *first* about Jew–Gentile hostility, and taking the biblical text seriously requires asking this question: What does it mean *today* for the New Testament to place so much importance on unity between Jewish and Gentile followers of Jesus?

History provides us with a third reason. The Christian churches have been guilty of a long chain of horrendous acts of anti-Semitism. When Gentile church leaders gained the upper hand in the third century, they first sidelined Jewish church leadership, then squashed it entirely. So there really is a dividing wall of hostility—including physical violence—between Gentile and Jewish followers of Jesus. None of us who are Roman Catholic, Eastern Orthodox, or Protestant can point our fingers at the other and claim innocence for ourselves. We are all guilty.[7]

---

6 For that matter, one way to view John 17 in light of subsequent history would be that Jesus prays first in verses 9–19 for the Jewish believers (represented by his disciples), and then in verses 20–26 for the Gentile believers (the vast majority of those who would believe through the gospel message brought to them by the Messianic Jews).

7 If you need convincing, or have courage from the Holy Spirit to delve more deeply into these difficult matters, I recommend that you purchase and read through *The LIST: Persecution of Jews by Christians throughout History*. This comprehensive book was compiled by Ray Montgomery and my friend and fellow Hope Chapel member Bob O'Dell. I challenge you to remain unmoved as you read example after example after example of Christian anti-Semitism.

But a silver lining to this dark cloud of history is emerging. We can discover a new posture of unity between Gentile Christians of all persuasions—namely, to kneel down together in lament before our Messianic Jewish brothers and sisters. We Protestant, Catholic, and Orthodox followers of Jesus find ourselves side-by-side, instead of against each other, as we jointly confess our sins and the sins of our forefathers. We are then united in Christ together with each other and with our new Messianic Jewish friends in the joy of restored relationship.

We found this joy frequently on the journey of repentance that was Wittenberg 2017.

Use the QR code or visit **https://bit.ly/w17ch13** to explore more pictures and additional material for this chapter, including my photo of the "League of Powerful Women."

Chapter 14

Antakya and Berlin

The most exhilarating experiences of my life have been those times when I have seen the kingdom of God being made real on earth. Such was Wittenberg 2017.

I vividly remember two events. They were like bookends: the beginning and the conclusion to the repentance process in Wittenberg.

In 2011, Thomas and Amy invited a small group of us from Antioch Network to walk the streets of Wittenberg and pray. We stopped and tilted our heads back to see the clearly visible Judensau sculpture high on the wall of the Stadtkirche. Still in shock, we turned to the nearby ancient open water channels still flowing along the streets in the middle of the town.

Bearing the pain of the degradation of religious contempt, we were thirsty for cleansing. Thomas suggested that Julia and I stand as Jews on one side of the water and the others, representing a variety of Christian traditions, stand on the opposite bank of the narrow channel. We prayed for each other in mourning for our history and then crossed the water, coming close together, calling on the Lord. As one, we yearned for the wider reconciliation.

In 2017, we were in Wittenberg once again. A large group of us, representing many Christian streams, walked through the streets. In humility before the Lord, we softly sang praises. I looked at the eyes of the local citizens. Surprised and curious, they stopped and stared. I watched as gradually expressions softened. Three of us led the procession: Peter, a dedicated Roman Catholic brother; Pfarrer Henning Dobers, a Protestant leader; and myself, a Messianic Jew. Peter and Henning took turns carrying the large wooden cross. Our crucified and risen Savior was the source of our unity.

HANNA MILEY, Anglican / Messianic Jew, survivor of the Holocaust, co-founder of Quellen, Phoenix, Arizona USA

Memories of Wittenberg 2017 for us:

Involvement of three generations also in the sense of Malachi 4:6.

Different ecumenical communities were hosting and serving us at four meetings.

Three highlights for us:

1) The identificational repentance prayer in St. Peter's Cathedral in Rome, built with money paid for indulgences.

2) Washing the feet of each other in the ancient church above Katakombe in Rome.

3) Reconciliation ceremony at the last meeting in Wittenberg 2017 with members of churches following the spiritual guidelines of the Anabaptist movement.

VERENA and HANS-PETER LANG, Charismatic Renewal in the Roman Catholic Church, Way of Reconciliation Austria, Austrian Round Table, Wieselburg, Austria

Wittenberg 2017 would not have happened without Hans-Peter and Verena Lang.

The Langs are Austrian Catholic charismatics. We first met them in 2010. We were in southern Turkey, in the city of Antakya (Antioch).

Antioch—where Luke reports that followers of "the Way" were first called "Christians."

Antioch—where a church of Jews and Gentiles formed outside of Jerusalem.

Antioch—where that church's diverse leadership team set aside Paul and Barnabas for the work to which the Holy Spirit was calling them.

Antioch—where an unbroken witness to the gospel of Jesus Christ has existed for almost two millennia.

Surprisingly, this was the first time that the Antioch Network had actually met in Antioch, the city. Amy and I flew with a friend into the small airport. We caught a taxi and tried to explain to the driver where we were going, using the directions that had been emailed to us. He nodded and set off, through suburbs of hastily constructed apartment buildings, under highway overpasses, and past restaurants and *kuafors*, where men were undergoing the time-honored Turkish tradition of getting groomed.

We could tell that we were penetrating into the heart of the ancient city as the side streets grew narrower and began to spring off at all angles. Suddenly, the taxi stopped. We got out. Where were we? We saw nothing familiar, except the entrance to what looked like a mosque. Surely the driver had brought us to the wrong place.

Nearby some children were happily playing street soccer. We approached them and showed them our directions. "Christians!" they said joyfully. Having identified us, they knew what to do. Down a narrow road past a dress shop, right, narrower still, then left to a dead end with a door. Knock, knock, knock … and the door opened to the face of a familiar friend. We tipped the kids, and I went back outside to join them for soccer in the streets. Thank God for the smiling Turkish children! Without them, we might still be wandering the back alleys of Antakya.

Some nuns from an Eastern Rite order had driven in from the west, and the next day we ended up at a lunch with them and a lovely couple from Austria, who turned out to be the Langs. We watched in amusement as the sister in charge discovered that she shared the Aramaic language in common with the waiter, proceeding thenceforth to order the most amazing meal of mezes—small Mediterranean dishes—and various meats with freshly made pita bread. Amy loves this kind of food … she was in heaven. At the end of the meal, everyone stood up, and it became clear that while ordering the food was in the purview of the nuns, paying for the food fell to Hans-Peter Lang. He graciously accepted the task, with a small smile that made me suspect this wasn't the first time.

Amy later described Hans-Peter as the grandfather everyone wants. His beard was soft, his eyes were always smiling, and his words were gentle. He had been a forester in Austria—a shepherd of the trees, as Tolkien describes the Ents. On any walk, when a tree needed identifying, Hans-Peter was sure to know.

Verena Lang was not gentle. She was a force of nature. I ended up leading the small group that Verena belonged to. I didn't realize the danger I was in! We were supposed to share prayer requests and then pray for each other. When it came to my turn, Verena did not even let me speak. She looked me square in the face and said:

"You are a workaholic, and it is going to kill you unless you deal with it."

What? Who was this woman?

I protested weakly, but Verena was having none of it. She gazed at me sternly, and with her open eyes fixed on me, she began to beseech God for me to not die yet. I knew that I had met a real person—someone with backbone and verve. I liked her immediately.

I liked her even more when the meeting's pivotal moment arrived. Most of the Protestant missionaries who were with us were somewhat confused by the presence of Roman and Eastern Rite Catholics, as well as by the liturgical prayer times that George Miley had organized. One day after a talk on the historic churches of the East, one of them hesitantly rose to his feet. "I guess I've never even thought about the historic churches in Turkey," he stammered … then sat down. Someone else began to speak on a different topic, but George firmly cut them off. "We have a person who is repenting of their disregard of the historic churches. This is important. Do we have anyone from the historic churches to receive this repentance?"

Verena's confident "We will" volunteered Hans-Peter as well. They came forward. George asked the Protestant to stand to before them and repeat his confession—to which he added, "I am sorry." The Langs looked in his eyes and said, "As Roman Catholics, we forgive you." They embraced … and the Holy Spirit swept through the room.

I thought to snap a quick picture with my iPhone of that first moment of reconciliation in Antakya. It remains one of the favorite photos I have ever taken.
Photo by Thomas Cogdell.

It felt like several hours later when the meeting finally ended. The Eastern Rite sisters had asked for forgiveness for their suspicion of overseas Protestant workers—while prostrated before them, kissing their feet. A young Baptist had expressed his lack of rootedness and been embraced by a Messianic Jewish father in the faith. To everyone's surprise, a visitor in the back of the room announced that he would return immediately to the Orthodox Church that he had left to ask forgiveness of his former friends. We were all overwhelmed by God's love pouring out through the words of repentance and forgiveness.

At dinner that night, Amy and I looked at each other in wonder. What had just happened? "A man could live his life for such a moment, and die completely satisfied," I remember saying, as Amy's eyes shone with love for God.

A year and a half later, we were together with the Langs again. This time we were in Berlin. A small leadership team was meeting up to explore together what God was doing in Europe.

Why were Americans even in the room? What had we to say on this topic?

At one point, George asked Amy and me to share our vision for Wittenberg 2017. I was expecting an enthusiastic reception from this group. But this time I had the response that George had long predicted—reserved reactions from quiet, thoughtful Germans and Austrians. Nobody jumped immediately on the bandwagon.

We Americans like immediate bandwagon jumpers! Of course, such a person is likely to transfer bandwagons many times, as their mood shifts. We don't like that so much.

The Langs were examining the bandwagon in private. The next day, they requested a meeting with us to talk about Wittenberg 2017. We didn't know what to think. We were nervous.

> We Americans like immediate bandwagon jumpers!

They drew out a neatly handwritten list of names, some crossed out, others added in the margins. "Here are the people we are willing to call on your behalf," Hans-Peter said. A Catholic archdeacon. A bishop. The longtime leader of the charismatic movement in Europe. Lutheran pastors. And the list went on. This was an even greater treasure map than the list of meeting rooms in Wittenberg.

Amy and I did not quite know how to respond. The Langs were willing to put their personal reputations on the line for two untested Americans with a vision and a room. This was a gift that could not be valued, only received.

We received it gratefully.

Over the course of the next year, through consultations with the entire Antioch Network council, we asked the Langs to be the official European leaders of Wittenberg 2017.

It was, perhaps, the best decision we made. Now Hans-Peter and Verena were not only on the bandwagon. They were in the driver's seat!

Verena and Hans-Peter in the lead! Photo by Thomas Cogdell.

Use the QR code or visit **https://bit.ly/w17ch14** to explore a map, more pictures, and additional material for this chapter, including St. Peter's Cave Church in Antioch, one of the oldest known Christian churches.

Chapter 15

Ottmaring, 2012

At my first ever Wittenberg 2017 meeting in Ottmaring, I arrived early and I had been asking God how I could engage with Wittenberg 2017. I saw an elderly lady wearing what I knew to be the dress of the Sisters of Mary. I thought, "Well, I wouldn't have much in common with her. Who else is here?" The Holy Spirit instantly said to me: "Go and buy her a coffee and a piece of cake!" I am so very glad that I obeyed immediately as Sister Joela is so full of Jesus, his wisdom, and God's spirit. She has been such a blessing and inspiration for me.

JULIA STONE, Jewish believer / Protestant nondenominational, Berlin, Germany

By faith Thomas and Amy obeyed when God called them, healing wounds in the body of Christ after 500 years. And they stepped out without asking for costs and through countless impossibilities, guiding us from far away, entering into the midst of deep traditional European conflicts of Christianity. No one of us would ever have dared this.

In the beginning I had no idea that Wittenberg 2017 would become an important chapter even in my life. To be short, I reduce this chapter into two moments:

1) In deep sadness, feeling helpless and lonely I was sitting on a bench of the huge Lateran-Basilica in Rome. Someone sat down beside me, prayed for me, and left me as quiet as he had come. It was Franziskus [Eisenbach].

2) In Trento I remember a time of purest heavenly joy singing again and again: "We are one in the Spirit, we are one in the Lord"!

Amy summarized my experiences during these years when she gave her last talk in Wittenberg about the glory of the bride in the glory of the cross.

SISTER JOELA KRÜGER, Marienschwestern (Evangelical Sisters of Mary–Lutheran), Darmstadt, Germany

"Are you the one who started all this trouble?"

The question was posed by a short but intimidating woman in a habit who had marched straight up to me after the train doors had swept open.

"Umm ... yes?" I meekly replied.

We were standing on the train platform of Ottmaring, the small German village where the Langs had called a meeting in 2012.

Ottmaring has a significant history in Protestant–Catholic reconciliation. In 1999, the Roman Catholic and Lutheran churches signed in Augsburg the Joint Declaration on the Doctrine of Justification, a remarkable document that effectively ended the original "protest" that sparked the Protestant Reformation.[1] In it, Lutherans and Catholics agreed upon a common approach to the theological question of justification by faith.

Those who participated in the actual signing in 1999 all stayed together at a retreat center run by the Focolare community. Founded by Chiara Lubich in 1943, the Focolare movement is a community dedicated to working for unity in the body of Christ. The Langs had booked this same retreat center for our meeting. Their wisdom was shown in choosing a place with a rich history of significant Catholic-Protestant reconciliation.

On the day before our meeting started, I was chosen to pick up an important member of the group at the train station. I don't know the reason I was selected, because I had never met Sister Joela Krüger. During one of our leadership calls, the Langs had reported being contacted by Sister Joela, a leader of the Marienschwestern. Amy and I had listened politely to their excitement—"We're not even sure how Sister Joela heard about it!" Since Marienschwestern means "Sisters of Mary" in German, we assumed they were a Catholic order. We were wrong.

The Marienschwestern of Darmstadt were Lutherans! Their founder was Mother Basilea Schlink, whose writings are well known even in the United States. She lived through the Allied bombing of Darmstadt during World War II, and even during that time she had protested the killing of Jews under the Nazi regime. When the war ended, she joined with a small band of similarly unmarried women to call their nation to repentance for the Holocaust. They formed a Lutheran order of nuns, highly respected

---

1 Use the QR code at the beginning of the book to read the text of the Joint Declaration.

not only in Germany but around the world. Their headquarters are in Darmstadt, but they developed branches in Jerusalem as well as nations such as Australia, Japan, Norway, and even the United States.

Mother Basilea died in 2001. Much of the leadership burden had then fallen to Sister Joela. For her to be coming to Ottmaring was, according to the Langs, simply amazing.

I stood on the platform, wondering if I would be able to figure out who she was. Train after train arrived, disgorging their passengers. I scanned the hurrying crowds for someone who looked like a "Sister Joela." What would I do if I had to go back to the Langs and report that I hadn't seen her?

But in the end I had no trouble recognizing her, because of course it was Sister Joela who confronted me and asked: "Are you the one who started all this trouble?"

After my timid affirmation, she fixed me with another penetrating stare: "Are there any Messianic Jews here?" This time I could answer strongly: "Yes!"

Thank God that Marianna, Hanna, and Julia were also in Ottmaring. I believe to this day that if I had said no, she would have turned around and gotten back on the train, and we wouldn't have ever seen her again.

Sister Joela holding our late-in-life surprise daughter, Clara, who was eight months old at Ottmaring. Photo by Thomas Cogdell.

The next morning, Amy and I were carrying our daughter Clara toward breakfast when Sister Joela met us at the top of the stairs. "Today, history will be made," she announced. We laughed. "If you say so …," we responded, and we really meant it. If someone like Sister Joela says that, you take it seriously.

The group that had gathered in Ottmaring had never been together before, and we had not met most of them. So to start off, Amy and I simply told our story. I mostly remember Amy sharing beautifully that day about her experience of the pain of God's heart. When I spoke, it was about misinterpreting the seven years, and bypassing the Wittenberg exit, and finally visiting Wittenberg to reserve the room. During that part I was so glad that Julia was our translator, since this had become her story as well.[2]

We finished. Then we were quiet. And we listened.

We listened as Verena Lang spoke about the sins of the Catholic Church leaders—*her* Catholic Church—during the years leading up to Martin Luther.

We listened as a holy silence fell in our midst.

We listened as that silence was pierced by a wail of grief. Our friend Sandi Pedrotti was on the floor, mourning the sins of the people of God.

We listened as Duane Grobman presented a powerful vision of worldwide impact for Wittenberg 2017.

We listened as Marianna Gol suggested 500 days of fasting leading up to the 500th anniversary.

We listened as Sister Joela proposed that we all meet again and invite others to join us.

And we listened at the very end, as—to our astonishment—George Miley rose to his feet. "God has chosen Thomas and Amy as the initiators of Wittenberg 2017. None of us know why he chose two Americans. But he did. We need to gather around them and pray for them as the leaders of Wittenberg 2017."

Amy and me? The leaders?

Amy and I had speculated before the meeting that someone there might know of a similar initiative that was German-led. If so, we would then hand off our room reservation and happily wait five years to attend their meeting. Or perhaps there wasn't anything else yet, and a leader would arise from this august group to take charge. And of course there was still the possibility that the group would set aside the entire vision as a nice idea, but not from God.

---

2 The skill of speaking while being translated was still new to us. You must think in short yet complete phrases—then stop! … just as you're getting going. I was learning to take advantage of the breaks, to consider more carefully my next words—or to offer up a quick prayer, "Lord, help me!"

But for the initiative to move forward with us as the leaders had not been on our list of possible outcomes. We were in a daze as the group gathered around us, laid their hands on our heads and shoulders, and prayed for God's blessing for our leadership and protection for our marriage.

During the plane ride home, we compared levels of amazement. Wittenberg was going to happen! Significant European leaders were on board. "I guess we need to cancel all of our plans for the next five years," Amy said to me. "It will take our full attention to lead Wittenberg 2017."

God must have laughed upon hearing that … because the events on the home front started accelerating as soon as the plane landed. But that is another story, for perhaps another book.

Use the QR code or visit **https://bit.ly/w17ch15** to explore a map, more pictures, and additional material for this chapter, including Duane Grobman's "earthquake/epicenter" vision.

Chapter 16

Volkenroda, 2013

Here I was at a conference of Protestant and Catholic Christians, speaking as a Messianic Jew—a Jewish believer in Yeshua (Jesus)—on the need for true reconciliation in his love. But in the midst of their concerns for unity within the body of Christ, here was I, having to come to terms, emotionally, spiritually, and theologically, with the depth of pain and suffering inflicted on my people by those who had been caught up in the horror of Nazism … So where to begin? We were there to meet for prayer, repentance, and confession in the run-up to Wittenberg 2017, the 500th anniversary of Martin Luther's nailing of ninety-five theses on the door of the Castle Church in Wittenberg, a small town over one hundred miles away. This event effectively launched the Protestant Reformation, which would change the face of Europe and the nature of the Church for centuries. The cornerstone of Luther's theology, that we are saved by grace through faith and not of our own good deeds or works of righteousness, is something with which I heartily concur. But the additional baggage of Luther's teachings, his many writings and sermons against the Jews, had done irreparable damage to Jewish–Christian relations.

RICHARD HARVEY, Messianic Jewish author, theologian, historian,
London, England

At the meeting in Kloster Volkenroda, there was this moment when we were praying with Benjamin Berger and he drew attention to the fact that the crucifix in the chapel, it having been torn down and vandalized but later recovered, reflected, in its mutilated state, the condition of the body of Christ since the Jew–Gentile split in the late second century and the innumerable divisions that had occurred since then. That, I thought, was the key moment of the whole meeting, simultaneously an affirmation of the need for a ministry like Wittenberg 2017 and a vision of the real nature and scope of the injury we have inflicted on the body of Christ—that is, on each other—with our divisions and bickering. The fact that the weather outside during this specific session was tempestuous and dark, starkly underscored that impression.

JOHN D. MARTIN, Pentecostal, Christ the Reconciler Community,
Koinonia Community, Biburg, Augsburg, Germany

Wittenberg 2017 was launched. We were the leaders. What should we do next? Ask the Langs, of course!

And Hans-Peter and Verena turned to Sister Joela. She was already setting the plan for the next meeting into motion.

First of all, Amy and I wondered why there should be another meeting before 2017. Why not just work toward the originally envisioned meeting on the 500th anniversary?

Hans-Peter and Verena listened patiently to these questions and explained to us: We needed to prepare for the 2017 meeting. It was a good thing we had five years ... that might be just enough.

Amy and I were able to accept this without really understanding it. In hindsight, the Langs were exactly right. What happened in 2017 would never have been possible without 2012, and 2013, and 2014, and 2015, and 2016.

Ok, we need meetings. We should go straight to Wittenberg, right?

Wrong again. Sister Joela chose an out-of-the-way German village called Volkenroda.

Well, we need a theme. Let's dive right into the deep issues of Catholic-Protestant reconciliation ... right?

Wrong a third time! The focus of the next meeting would be German Lutheran repentance for anti-Semitism. Once again, we had questions: what does this have to do with Martin Luther? But once again, we trusted the Langs, and they trusted Sister Joela.

> Is anything more valuable in a leadership team than trust?

Is anything more valuable in a leadership team than trust? Books are written on strategy, structure, financial stability, effective communication, and a thousand other leadership topics. But what did Jesus say to his leadership team? "I no longer call you servants, because a servant does not know what his master is doing. Instead, I call you friends, because everything I have learned from my Father I have made known to you" (John 15:15).[1]

---

1 And this was before the scattering, before the betrayal, before the denials, before the cross, before Pentecost. Jesus trusted weak, immature, broken men who were about to fall and fail in dramatic ways.

George Miley was already working to teach us about "apostolic bands"—like the band of leaders that formed around the apostle Paul to take the gospel into new territory. One aspect of an apostolic band, George taught, was that the leaders were mutually submitted to one another.[2]

"You must trust the Langs," George would tell us. "They know what you don't know, and they have insight into the unique situation in Europe. Trust them." So we did.

We had also learned from George that repentance must be received.[3] So, who in the 2013 meeting would receive the repentance of German Lutherans concerning anti-Semitism? Why, Messianic Jews, of course!

We began to understand the urgency of Hans Wiedenmann, Hans Scholz, and Sister Joela—"Where are the Jews? Are they involved?"

For this meeting, two more Messianic Jews would be added to our company. One was Benjamin Berger. Benjamin was one of the very first of the modern Messianic Jews. In the 1960s, he had an unexpected spiritual encounter with Yeshua that convinced him that he had found the Messiah. He now lived in Jerusalem. The other was Richard Harvey. Richard was a historian and theologian who lived in London.[4]

When Father Peter Hocken heard that Marianna, Benjamin, and Richard would all be at the upcoming meeting, he expressed surprised pleasure. "Do you realize how unusual it is for these three to be at the same meeting?"

Once in Volkenroda, I made a point of seeking out both Benjamin and Richard to welcome them on the first night. Benjamin thanked me graciously. Richard examined me with a very British look and informed me that he wasn't sure why he was even here. I was both intimidated and enchanted by him.

My mother also came to this meeting. Her name is Ann Cogdell. She was born in Vermont on October 3, 1940. She was a concert pianist who had given up her promising career to raise me and my two sisters.

---

2 This mutual submission was very different than the top-down organizational structure of most ministries we had seen, where the person at the top gives the direction—perhaps having considered the input of his or her subordinates—and they execute these orders. Top-down leadership is, of course, an appropriate structure in many contexts.

3 George had halted the Antakya meeting in 2010 when he heard an expression of repentance, in order to ask who could receive it.

4 I learned later that Richard had written *Mapping Messianic Jewish Theology*, the first book on the various threads of theology in the reemerging Messianic Jewish tradition.

With my mother at the Volkenroda gathering. Photo by Ryan and Noleen Thurman. Used with permission.

Mom had traveled to Austria as a child to study piano for a year in a prestigious Salzburg conservatory. She had always treasured those memories, and when I invited her and my father, John to the Volkenroda meeting, her face lit up. My dad decided not to come, and Amy could not make this meeting either, so the Cogdell clan was represented by my mother and me.

One night, we went for a long walk together on the roads that ran through and around the small town. She showed me the pottery studio that she had wandered into earlier detailing her connection with the artist and the pottery she had purchased. She opened her heart to talk about her life, her feelings, her marriage, her motherhood—as never before, and never afterward. She talked about the pain in her heart, and the longing for her true self to finally emerge. I mostly listened, not really knowing how to respond, except to let her know that I was hearing her, and that I cared.

Looking back, my eyes fill with tears as I write this. I understand even more fully how God was weaving his tapestry in those days.

The three pioneers of reconciliation in Germany (left to right): Friedrich Aschoff, Furst Castell, and Franziskus Eisenbach. Photo by Thomas Cogdell.

Amy and I were always given the honor of opening each meeting, which was a reciprocal act of trust from the European leaders. Since Amy wasn't in Volkenroda, I spoke alone. All I could think to speak about was the Bible that Julia and I had seen in Luther's pulpit in 2010, which had been opened to that strange, blank page between the Old and New Testaments. Of course, for me, the blank page was preparatory to the main point—turning over a new page to John 17.

But after I finished speaking, Friedrich Aschoff asked to address the group. Who is Friedrich Aschoff? A dignified, elderly Lutheran pastor, Friedrich formed a team with two others to spearhead reconciliation efforts in Germany in the 1990s.[5]

Friedrich opened his Bible and read the last verse of the Old Testament:

> See, I will send the prophet Elijah to you before that great and dreadful day of the Lord comes. *He will turn the hearts of the fathers to their children, and the hearts of the children to their fathers*; or else I will come and strike the land with a curse. (Mal 4:5–6; emphasis added, NIV 1984)

Then he turned the page to the first verse of the New Testament:

> This is the book of the genealogy of Jesus the Messiah (Christ), *the son of David, the son of Abraham.* (Matt 1:1; emphasis added)

Then he spoke:

> *I believe that the blank page that the Bible was open to in Luther's pulpit, was no accident. God was giving us a message. That message was that the hearts of the fathers must turn to the children, and the hearts of the children to the fathers. Matthew answers Malachi's prophetic cry with Jesus—the Son of the heavenly Father, but also the son of a Jewish mother. This turning of the hearts must also become reality for us, in this room, and for this movement.*

The hearts of the fathers … of the parents … of the mothers—turning to the children. And the children's hearts turning back to them.

This is what was happening as my mother and I walked the streets of Volkenroda. It was a small, hidden moment. But it was a precursor to much larger fulfillments yet to come.

Since then, Friedrich's word has settled more and more deeply into my heart. It is one key to the complicated set of locks that is the divided body of Christ. For example, who are the fathers and mothers of the Protestants?

---

5 Remarkably, these other two were also present in our small gathering in Volkenroda: Franziskus Eisenbach, auxiliary bishop emeritus of Mainz; and Furst Castell, a respected member of the German nobility.

> It is one key to the complicated set of locks that is the divided body of Christ.

Well, certainly the Catholics. What if the hearts of the Catholics turned to the Protestants—suddenly proud of their children in the faith, urging them onward in their pursuit of the kingdom of God? And what if the hearts of the Protestants turned back to their Catholic heritage—acknowledging their preservation and propagation of the gospel, thanking them for their faithfulness through century after century before the Protestant witness to the gospel had been birthed?

O Holy Spirit, hasten the day when the hearts of the children are turned to the parents, and the parents to the children!

One aspect of this turning of the hearts is honor. It is so important to honor. Honor does not mean blind praise or triumphalism. A person can, indeed must, honor their parents—even if their parents have sinned against them. A realistic appraisal of the faults of the parents goes hand in hand with honor.

As a nondenominational Christian, I have learned to honor Martin Luther as one of my fathers in the faith. I have certainly learned more about his failings than I ever imagined. And I have gained a greater appreciation for the necessary understandings he made clear in his clarion call for reform.

Who are your fathers and mothers in the faith? How can you accord them the honor they are due?

> Honor your father and your mother, as the Lord your God commanded you, that your days may be long, and that it may go well with you in the land that the Lord your God is giving you. (Deut 5:16; ESV)

And who are the parents of the Roman Catholic Church? The Messianic Jews![6] What if the Catholics saw themselves as birthed out of the Messianic movement and daringly realized that perhaps Rome was not the ultimate authority in Christendom? And what if the Messianic Jews—who almost to a person are bitter toward the Catholics from centuries of persecution—instead realized that the Roman Catholics were their children in the faith, born not of human will, but of the will of God?

---

6 Our Eastern Orthodox brothers and sisters might insert themselves between the Roman Catholics and Messianic Jews, but the same principle would then hold for them.

Such a turning of the hearts would require a deep work of repentance, which was the reason that the Langs and Sister Joela had chosen this location for our meeting. Volkenroda was in the heart of Thuringia. Thuringia was the location of Luther's childhood and education. And nearby was Eisenach, the former home of the Nazi De-Judification Institute.

Sister Joela explained this institute during her afternoon talk. The Nazis had decided to remove all references to the Jewish people from German culture, to strip them of any meaningful identity. So in 1939, they—or rather, the German Lutheran Church as their proxy—created the De-Judification Institute. One of its main projects was to strip all mentions of Israel and the Jews from the Bible.

What kind of Bible would be left? A Nazi Bible. A Bible that the Reich would give to German Lutheran churches, with orders to read and preach only from it. A sacrilege.

Sister Joela finished her talk, and we walked in silent procession to the Volkenroda chapel. The crucifix in this chapel had been found in some rubble from the original thirteenth-century monastery. It was Christ, battered. The arms were removed, and a large part of his head was dented in. We formed a circle around this crucifix and began to mourn.

Repentance in the Volkenroda chapel. Photo by Thomas Cogdell.

The previous day, I had posed a vulnerable and very serious question to Richard Harvey—"Teach me how to mourn."

"Oh, the Jews know how to mourn," he replied. "In fact, we've written a book on it," he went on. My pen was poised, ready to write down the title of this mysterious volume. "It's called … Lamentations," he concluded, with a twinkle in his eye.

So I read Lamentations. One of the things that I noticed was the mention of tearing the garments as an expression of mourning.

As we knelt in the chapel, I looked down at my garment. I was wearing one of my favorite shirts. It was a bright orange Patagonia base layer, which I liked to pull on as a sweater. It was perfect for the crisp, fall weather in central Germany. I tore it. I tore it again. I didn't tear it because I felt grief. I tore it to feel grief, as a discipline of mourning. I tore it to enter a world that I had always avoided. I tore it three times.

Then someone added a Jewish prayer shawl to the broken body on the crucifix. We were all invited to come and kneel, as an act of repentance for the Gentile church forgetting that Jesus was a Jew. I stood in line. I knelt, in my torn shirt.

What was going on?

We could all recognize that this was a holy moment. Marianna, Benjamin, and Richard came forward. They received our repentance, offered us gracious words of forgiveness, and we all embraced.

But … what was going on?

The next day, Richard Harvey offered some insight:

> I didn't know why I came here. But as I arrived, I saw a rainbow from my car window, and knew I was in the right place. And now I know why. I must write a book about Martin Luther, from the perspective of a Messianic Jew, for the 500th anniversary. There will be many books from many different perspectives that will be published leading up to 2017. But none of them will address him from a Jewish point of view. My book will.

And he wrote that book. *Luther and the Jews* was published in the summer of 2017. Here's how it ends:

> I'm looking for the *Hora* [a Jewish circle dance] to break out in heaven and catch everyone up in its swirling excitement. So let's get dancing today! I want to see the *Hora* wherever the anniversary of Luther is celebrated, so that Jews, Germans, and Jewish believers in Jesus can dance together. I want to see us singing and dancing with the words *havenu shalom aleichem* ("we bring you peace") and *hineh mah tov umanaim shevet achim gam yahad* ("behold how good and how pleasant it is when brothers and sisters dwell together in unity"). Only then will Luther's dream of the kingdom of God on earth be established. "Not by might, nor by power, but by my spirit, says the Lord" (Zechariah 4:6).

Richard's hopeful vision would prove to be prophetic.

Use the QR code or visit **https://bit.ly/w17ch16** to explore a map, more pictures, and additional material for this chapter, including what made John Porterfield exclaim, "I've just walked through the wardrobe door!"

Chapter 17

Trento, 2014

Having the opportunity to work with several ministries focused on Christian unity, I am convinced that effectiveness is tied inextricably to the commitment of the leadership to model unity and humility amongst themselves. I had the privilege of being part of the Wittenberg 2017 leadership team. We were convinced our primary responsibilities were providing spiritual covering and protecting the unity of the work. Throughout our time together, God gave us grace to submit to Christ and to one another, and we can testify how we saw and experienced God manifest his healing power and the ministry of reconciliation among and through us.

RYAN THURMAN, Anglican, International Director of Antioch Network, Phoenix, Arizona USA

For us Wittenberg 2017 started a whole new season in our life (actually in our whole family's life) in which God's blessing was released in a new and amazing way. Through the friendships that evolved from our involvement and the experience of repentance and reconciliation, God led us in a deeper and more profound understanding of his love and mercy. We were especially impressed with the way the leadership of the Wittenberg 2017 movement handled different challenges and relational struggles during the meetings. Particularly we recall the Shabbat celebration in the 2014 meeting in Trento, when everyone responded with humility and maturity to Richard Harvey, who felt offended by the way the tallit was treated during the celebration—although he himself reacted in a very mature way as well. We really learned a lot from our involvement in the team and the whole movement.

LUDWIG and CECILY BENECKE, Evangelical Lutheran (Ludwig) and Roman Catholic (Cecily), co-founders of Quellen, Trieb, Germany

When the first moment of public disagreement came, dread from the pit of my stomach crawled up to freeze my mind. I had to respond immediately. I stood up and slowly made my way to the microphone at the front of the room. I had no idea what I was going to say.

Conflict is inevitable in works of reconciliation.

For one thing, reconciliation addresses hostility. It requires bringing differing parties with histories of hostility into one place, to meet together. The atmosphere can be charged with tension.

By God's grace, this was rarely the case in the Wittenberg 2017 meetings. There was a high degree of maturity in all of the participants—they had allowed themselves to be formed more and more into the image of Jesus. They were people of humility, patience, humor, and love. Love covers a multitude of sins.

A second consideration is the evil intentions of God's enemy. The devil is always attacking relationships, seeking to divide and conquer. As Jesus pointed out—a house divided against itself cannot stand. This is particularly true when the "house" is an initiative seeking to unify the broken body of Christ. The enemy of Christ rages against this and ramps up the intensity of the assault.

George Miley helped us immensely as the leadership team was forming. He would ask us: "What is the primary task of the leadership team?"

We would offer up the traditional answers—"to make decisions," "to strategize," "to move the project forward toward its goal," "to ensure financial stability and integrity," and the like. And George would acknowledge that these are important *secondary* responsibilities.

And then George would answer his own question:

> The primary task of the leadership team is to protect the unity of the leadership team.

At first, George's answer puzzled me. It seemed self-referential, inward focused, and unproductive. George kept trying to explain—"If the parents are unified, then the children are at peace." More than grasping this with my mind, I trusted George's spiritual wisdom with my heart—so I watched and waited to see how it played out.

We formulated the following practices as a concrete way to protect our unity:

- When faced with a decision to make, we listen to each person on the team. This includes recognizing that some will be reticent to speak out, or if they do speak out, might hesitate to speak their mind honestly. So we inquire further whenever we suspect we are not fully hearing someone's heart and mind in the matter.

- If everyone is clearly in agreement, we say "Yes" together and move forward in the decision.
- If we are not all in agreement, we don't say "Yes" … but we also don't say "No." We simply wait."

This rule proved difficult for me. I am accomplished in both the "Ready—Fire—Aim" and the "Ask forgiveness, not permission" modes of leadership.[1] I am an action person. I feel most comfortable when I am on the move. I have had many wonderful mentors tell me that it's better to act, even wrongly, than to not act at all. So on many leadership calls, when I felt I could see the right direction to go, and not everyone on the team was there with me … I would submit, but with difficulty. I had to stop myself many times from expressing my frustration, not because it would not have been heard and responded to well, but because I would not have said it well in my own immaturity. I could have easily damaged the team.

In the end, I came to see that George was so wise in this area. He understood that the enemy's primary attack against Wittenberg 2017 would be to divide the leadership team. Any given action or decision, even a right one, that resulted in a slight wedge between team members would then be pounded on with the enemy's sledgehammer until the crack became a gulf, and the initiative would fall to pieces. Better not to make the right decision, than to make it in disunity. Or, to say it another way—if we were not in agreement, to *not* make the "right decision" *was* in fact the right decision. We adhered to this rule year after year during the planning of all the preparatory meetings. When 2017 rolled around and we were faced with many momentous decisions, we were able to quickly come to agreement because we all trusted one another. I am now convinced that true trust is a rare currency of the highest value in leadership.

So the conflict that arose during the Trento meeting in 2014 was not among the leadership team, because of the protection of God through George's counsel. But the conflict was quite public. Here's what happened.

Amy had prepared an exercise based on a passage written by Father Raniero Cantalamessa:

---

1 I still believe these are appropriate approaches in some contexts.

> *The church is like water: it "weighs" the bodies that fall into it. Those that have solidity and substance sink down into the water's depths, perhaps slowly, but the water receives them. Those that are empty and lack substance are pushed back up to the surface.[2]*

Amy was captivated by this picture likening gifts from the various traditions to weights that sink into the depths of the church. So she brought some pearls to Trento. And a bowl for the water. Our plan was to have those from different ecclesial communities—Anglican, Catholic, Baptist, charismatic, Messianic Jewish, Presbyterian, and so forth—get into groups and determine what "pearls" they brought to the body of Christ that had "solidity and substance." They would drop these pearls into the bowl, where they would be "received" by the water, joining with pearls from others to enrich the whole people of God.

In preparing the table in front for the exercise, we thought it would be meaningful to show in some way that God had built the Christian church upon a Jewish foundation. The symbol that we—the small group preparing the exercise, which included Marianna Gol, a Messianic Jew—chose was to place the bowl of water on top of a Jewish prayer shawl, or tallit. As the pearls sank down one by one, the Jewish roots would thus be visible beneath them.

Richard wearing the Jewish prayer shawl, or tallit, during a prayer.
Photo by Jo Hoffman. Used with permission.

After a wonderful time of morning worship, we placed the shawl on the table, with the bowl of water on top, and began to explain the exercise with the pearls. Suddenly, a loud voice rose up from the midst of those who were seated. It was Richard Harvey.

"I object! The Jewish prayer shawl is NOT a tablecloth. You can NOT use it like that."

As soon as he said this, a wail arose from the far side of the room. It was Marianna Gol, reacting to Richard's outcry. Later, she told us the feelings that came over her in that moment—that while Richard may have been

---

2 From *Contemplating the Trinity*, by Raniero Cantalamessa OFM CAP, chapter 6, section 4, p. 105.

technically right, for him to object publicly in this manner grieved her. Amy, Verena, and one of the Marienschwestern sisters immediately got up from their seats and went over to be with Marianna.

Now a third strong voice—this time belonging to Richard's friend Johannes Fichtenbauer, the archdeacon of the diocese of Vienna: "Richard, I appreciate what you are saying. I agree with you about the prayer shawl. But, you have NO RIGHT to oppose this symbol."

The eyes in the room had swung from the stage to Richard. Then from Richard to Marianna. Then from Marianna to Johannes. And now from Johannes to me.

> Was this the moment when the whole Wittenberg initiative would fall apart?

I knew I had to say something. I had no idea what I was going to say. I got up and went hesitantly to the microphone. Dread was in the pit of my stomach. My steps were slow and my thoughts were fearful. Was this the moment when the whole Wittenberg initiative would fall apart?

I opened my mouth, and listened as words emerged: "Richard, I am so sorry that we have offended you. This was not our intention. I personally ask for your forgiveness. Will you forgive me?"

"Yes, I forgive you." (Whew! I was very grateful at that moment that Richard's generous spirit matched his Jewish forthrightness.) "But you still can't use the prayer shawl like that."

Hmmm ... what to do? I opened my mouth again, curious to see what would come out this time.

"Let's take a break. We'll decide how to proceed, and then start up again in one hour."

All of this happened in Trento, Italy. We were well hosted again by the Focolare, this time at their motherhouse—a beautiful facility built into the side of an Alpine mountain. The European leadership team chose Trento because it had been the site of the post-Reformation Council of Trent. That council had addressed many of the questions raised by Martin

Luther. And it had ended with a pronouncement of "anathem"a on the new "Protestants."[3]

Upon arrival, three greetings from outside our group greatly encouraged us. The first was from the mayor of Trento, welcoming us into the city. In the second, the local Roman Catholic bishop informed us that to his knowledge, we were the first ever Protestant–Catholic reconciliation gathering in Trento. The third was a warm message from Cardinal Christoph Schönborn, OP, archbishop of Vienna.

Verena Lang's talk on the second day was monumental. She spoke as an Austrian PhD in history as well as a loyal Roman Catholic who loved her Church. She honored Martin Luther. Here is a summary of her message:

> Martin Luther was a prophet.
>
> He was not a rebel. He was a faithful Roman Catholic, an Augustinian monk, professor of theology in a leading university. The image of Luther defiantly nailing his Ninety-Five Theses onto the door of the church in Wittenberg is not supported by historical facts. It is a legend. And it is an unhelpful legend, because it gives the wrong picture of Luther in 1517. Martin Luther was acting appropriately as a prophetic voice to his own church. He was not intending to divide the church when he sent this message. Instead, he correctly submitted it to the apostolic authority that was over him in the church hierarchy.
>
> It is known for certain that he mailed the Ninety-Five Theses to Albrecht, the archbishop of Mainz. He then waited for Albrecht's reply, expecting an honest theological discussion to ensue. What did Albrecht of Mainz do? Did he correctly handle the prophetic word that he received? No, he did not. He did not respond to Martin Luther at all. Instead, he forwarded the theses to Pope Leo X, for him to censure Martin Luther.

Verena then presented a very helpful picture. A happy church building was well supported by two equally strong pillars. One pillar bore the label "Apostolic"; the other, "Prophetic." She explained that this depicted Paul's statement that God's household is "built on the foundation of the apostles and prophets, with Jesus Christ being the chief cornerstone" (Eph 2:20).

She then displayed another picture of the same church building. But in this one, the apostolic pillar had grown much larger, pushing up the

---

3 Anathema is a formal curse of excommunication upon a person, group, or doctrine that is considered particularly loathsome.

church building on one side. On the other side, the pillar representing the prophetic had deteriorated and was crumbling away beneath the weight being placed on it as the church tilted over. The building was toppling, oversupported on one side and undersupported on the other.

This was the situation in my church in 1517. The church was unbalanced. The apostolic had grown overly important, and the prophetic voice went unheard. It was a true tragedy. It ended in division, when Pope Leo excommunicated Martin Luther.

Verena's diagram of the two pillars. Photo by Verena Lang. Used with permission.

Then Verena paused. She bowed her head, and wept. She wept for her own church, grieving this dark moment in its history. And every heart—Catholic, Protestant, Jewish—was moved by her grief.

That evening, we gathered for prayer in a beautiful, round chapel. A slight, dignified man arose to speak. His name was Franziskus Eisenbach.

I am a Roman Catholic priest. I am auxiliary bishop emeritus for the city of Mainz. In a certain way, I sat in the same seat as Albrecht, who was bishop of Mainz centuries before me. On behalf of my predecessor, I repent to God before all of you. Albrecht did not listen to the voice of the young prophet Martin Luther. He protected himself instead of seeking the heart of God. What he did was wrong. I ask those of you who are Lutherans in the room tonight to forgive me, and to forgive him.

Then Franziskus knelt on the hard, stone floor.

Burkard and Franziskus embrace.
Photo by Thomas Cogdell.

Suddenly, a figure was kneeling beside him. It was Burkard Hotz, a Lutheran pastor. And there, in the city of the Council of Trent, where Roman Catholic bishops had declared all German Lutherans to be "anathema," a Roman Catholic bishop and a German Lutheran pastor were exchanging the embrace of love and forgiveness. And we could all sense the healing balm of the Holy Spirit covering ancient sins that had divided Protestants and Catholics for centuries.

The world is not worthy of such beauty.

That was one of the pivotal acts of reconciliation in the entire Wittenberg 2017 journey.

That the conflict between Richard and Marianna happened *after* this important moment demonstrates that no victory in reconciliation will go unchallenged by our spiritual enemy, who hates the unity of the Trinity.

So ... what happened with the exercise of the pearls?

In the hour break that we took, delegates from the leadership team went back and forth to Richard and Marianna. Our first concern was their relationship. That was more important than the meeting or any other part of our plans. When a wound opens, triage takes first priority. We saw that emotions were running too high for Marianna and Richard to talk together in the moment. But both of them committed to meet together at a later time and seek reconciliation.[4]

---

4 Jesus commands that among brothers and sisters direct address should be practiced: when there is a rift in a relationship, you are to go and try to resolve it rather than waiting, hiding, or overlooking the offense. These actions of reconciliation can be found in Jesus's dual statements recorded in Matthew 5 and Matthew 18, which together make it clear that you should go whether you are the offended one or the offender.

We also arrived at a compromise with the prayer shawl, agreed to by both of them. We would fold the prayer shawl up and place it beside the bowl. This would still communicate the importance of the Jewish roots, without dishonoring the tallit.

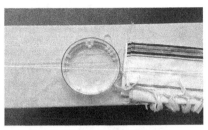

The Jewish prayer shawl next to—not underneath—the pearls.
Photo by Thomas Cogdell.

In the end, the exercise exceeded our expectations. As each group shared, it turned into the most joyful—even hilarious—time! Some groups had trouble proceeding because they were overcome by laughter. I believe God gave that lightness as a consolation for the tension we had suffered earlier in the day.

Looking back, I am thankful for the difficult trial of our first major conflict.[5] It showed us the possibility of expressing a strongly emotional reaction without destroying unity. It also showed us how important symbols are, and how different people can interpret the same symbol differently—even people from the same tradition.

I am even thankful that the conflict was public. I believe it was somehow helpful for the entire group to see that when conflict inevitably arises in a reconciliation initiative, Jesus has already given us the way to respond—with humility, with direct address, with forgiveness, and with mutual attentiveness to the Holy Spirit.

Use the QR code or visit **https://bit.ly/w17ch17** to explore a map, more pictures, and additional material for this chapter, including a video of some of the presentations from the exercise with the pearls.

---

5 When Richard read my account of this, his lovely response was: "With my English understatement I would call it a 'disagreement' or 'difference of views' rather than a 'conflict'... for us as Jewish people I would say it was pretty mild. Real conflict is when we go at each other like cats and dogs, but still end up being the best of friends!"

Chapter 18

Rome, 2015

The worship service we held together on October 25 in Rome is a very special memory to me. We celebrated it as a "pre-Eucharistic" thanksgiving service with foot washing. I found this very moving, because the foot washing was a visible expression of the servant love of Jesus that we have the privilege of demonstrating to each other. This servant love of our Lord is the wonderful foundation of Christian ecumenism and the basis for overcoming divisions. This became clear to me as a deeply moving certainty in this worship service that followed our visit to the Catacombs.

BURKARD HOTZ, pastor, Evangelical Lutheran Church,
Wiesloch, Germany

The five years that I could be part of Wittenberg 2017 were a very special time for me personally, which probably shaped my entire life. The excellent talks on the various topics were very illuminating and helped formulate a concrete confession. The honesty, love, and readiness for reconciliation among the participants who faced up to the guilt of their respective denominations—that made it easy to face these difficult topics. One high point for me was the time in St. Peter's Cathedral, where we, in tears, confessed the guilt of our Catholic Church, and the other denominations then confessed theirs. This was a powerful work of the Holy Spirit like I have rarely experienced.

BR. PIETRO BERGERHOFER, Roman Catholic,
member of the Franciscan Brothers who serve/work alongside
the Marienschwestern (Evangelical Sisters of Mary–Lutheran),
Darmstadt, Germany

There was a good reason back in 1517 for Albrecht, the bishop of Mainz, to resist Luther's message.

Albrecht had *purchased* his bishopric. This was illegal according to the rules of the Catholic Church—and yet, in fact, he had purchased not one but *three* bishoprics. So he was the bishop in three different dioceses, which also violated the rules.

Why had Albrecht bought his way into being a bishop? It was not from a desire to shepherd God's people. His motives were money and power.

But Albrecht was in debt. He had borrowed 29,000 guilders for these purchases, the equivalent of multiple millions of dollars. The Fuggers of Augsburg, who were the dominant bankers of Europe, would be expecting repayment.

So Albrecht worked out a plan with Pope Leo X to cover his debts. His plan? To sell indulgences to the German people, under the promise that this would release their dead relatives from purgatory. Of course, the sale of spiritual benefits also was illegal according to church law. But that didn't stop Albrecht or his salesman Johann Tetzel, whose famous marketing slogan was:

> As soon as the gold in the casket rings
> The rescued soul to heaven springs.

The deal called for 50 percent of the proceeds to stay with Albrecht, so that he could pay off his debt and then begin to reap a profit. The other half would be sent to Rome.

What was the money sent to Rome from Germany used for?

Pope Leo X had inherited a major building project. His predecessor, Pope Julius II, had turned his eyes on the historic church housing Peter's tomb in Rome. Pope Julius deemed the building to be too small for such a noble purpose. Since Peter was the rock upon which the church was built, Pope Julius's goal was to replace the church with a structure whose grandeur matched its name—St. Peter's Basilica.

When Pope Julius died, the plans had already been set in motion for the largest church building in the world.[1] It was to be furnished with the finest of Renaissance art—including Michelangelo's famous statue, the *Pietà*. Pope Leo X was now responsible for carrying this vision to completion.

And the money for this flowed from Germany. A substantial portion of the financing for the construction of St. Peter's came from Albrecht's sale of indulgences.

The very indulgences that Luther's Ninety-Five Theses denounced.

---

1 St. Peter's Basilica remains the largest church building in the world.

So when Albrecht received Luther's prophetic message, it wasn't merely an academic discussion to him. It threatened to pull out the bottom from his financial house of cards. No indulgences, no debt payments.

And when Pope Leo received the message from Albrecht, passing along the writings of the young German monk, he too was not able to respond in the proper theological or pastoral manner. After all, what would be the impact on his building project? No indulgences, no St. Peter's.

Both of the apostolic authorities over Luther, Albrecht, and Leo, had been compromised by financial entanglements. Threatened by Luther's prophetic word, they bent their considerable resources to silence him.

"... you who kill the prophets and stone to death those sent to you!"

> A few steps in, Amy grabbed my arm and began to sob.

Our group knew this history as we entered through the Holy Door into St. Peter's Basilica. Many thousands of tourists surrounded us. A few steps in, Amy grabbed my arm and began to sob. I held her tightly. Verena came to support her from the other side, but she too began to weep and was assisted in turn by her son Georg. Slowly, somberly, we processed up past ornate side chapels and marvelously beautiful colonnades.

Franziskus had written ahead and requested one of the side chapels for our meeting. But he had not heard back. Now he was off making inquiries with the church authorities. He returned as we reached the center of the church, with the vast dome high overhead.

"All of the chapels are full, but they have given us a place to meet. Come with me."

He opened the door in the altar rail behind Peter's tomb, and the noisy crowds melted away. We were alone, protected from sight, in a sanctuary of silence at the heart of St. Peter's. The Lord had truly prepared this place for us.

Franziskus began to speak. He read slowly through the story of Jesus cleansing the temple in John 2. He began to repent for the love of money and fear of men that had clouded the judgments of Albrecht and Pope Leo.

Repentance in St. Peter's Basilica, which was built with the proceeds from the indulgences that Martin Luther protested. Photo by Ryan and Noleen Thurman. Used with permission.

We all knelt or prostrated ourselves. I felt the cold marble against my cheek as I held out my phone to record what was happening. Had anyone, in all of the history of this building, ever repented here? Had the truth ever been confessed within these walls—that part of the price paid for the grandeur of St. Peter's was a dividing wound in the body of Christ?

We all sensed the ears of heaven, attentive to the prayers being lifted up. The Holy Spirit filled each of us with a strange mixture of sorrow and awe.

Suddenly, Franziskus no longer stood alone. One of the Lutheran pastors joined him.

"What Franziskus is confessing is not a Catholic problem. It is a Christian problem. It is our problem. We Lutherans, too, harden our hearts to the voice of the prophets when they challenge our financial practices and building projects. We, too, must repent."

Then Edi stood up and walked over. Edi Griesfelder was the leader of the Pentecostals in Austria.

"Father, as a representative of the Protestant Free Churches, I'd like to ask your forgiveness for where the leaders, founders of churches, just as here in this place, maybe they didn't abuse the money of their people, but they abused their time and their zeal, to build their own kingdom, rather than to build your kingdom. Father, have mercy and forgive us."

And there they stood, in the heart of St. Peter's: a Catholic priest, a Lutheran pastor, and a Pentecostal preacher.[2] All our hearts were joined to theirs as they wept, grieved, and embraced each other. In that most glorious sanctuary of Western civilization, we brought to Jesus one at a time our weakness, our sins, our failings, and our divisions.

One member of our group from the Baptist tradition wrote afterward:

So on bent knee the bishop bowed himself before God and those who were there and asked for forgiveness. Confessing the sins of his tradition, he lamented the fact that what was meant for a house of prayer had been built upon the abuses of indulgences to testify to the legacy of men. As he confessed, and as the other Catholics within the group joined him in their shared sorrow, it was as though the Spirit was showing each of us how this history was not just the history of Catholics, but was our shared history. This confession led to our united plea for healing and restoration.

The abuse of the indulgences belongs to the Western tradition, and it is this tradition that the Protestant movement arose out of and from, and is also indebted to. As a Protestant, and more so as an Evangelical and a Baptist, it became very evident that the sins of arrogance and greed were not isolated to the Catholic tradition and the indulgences.[3]

Finally, the time that had been given us was over. Sensing the holiness of the moment lift, we slowly arose, then began to walk out. There was a hush in our midst. I couldn't resist joining in with a few who had their phones out, snapping pictures in that special place. And then back down the vast nave, one last photo of the *Pietà*, and out into the sunshine of St. Peter's

---

2 The Lutheran pastor was Hans Scholz. He later wrote a beautiful reflection on the Rome gathering (see appendix 6).

3 http://www.a2jphoenix.org/blog/wittenberg-2017-the-bent-knee-of-humility

Square.[4] The sun was going down, the sky was crystal blue, and the air was clear. We took a group photo in the lovely Rome evening, and then slowly dispersed, walking away in small groups, heading on to restaurants or back to hotels, each with our own thoughts.

Nobody who was there that day will ever forget the time in St. Peter's.

Neither, I believe, will the hosts of heaven.

> Then those who feared the LORD talked with each other, and the LORD listened and heard. A scroll of remembrance was written in his presence concerning those who feared the LORD and honored his name. (Mal 3:16)

We encountered two more surprises of the Holy Spirit in Rome: increasing numbers of youth and of German nobility. These two groups were both represented in the young German couple Ludwig and Cecily Benecke, who each came from a noble family.[5]

I hate to paint with too broad a brush, but many Christian reconciliation gatherings feature the wizened theologians, the war-weary intercessors, and the white-haired pastors and bishops. Not that we don't need the fathers and mothers of the faith—they are indispensable and their work is worthy of honor. But we also need to "listen to the youth," as Saint Benedict posited centuries ago and Father Roger of Taizé often repeated last century.

When planning the Rome meeting, we observed with joy, and a little bemusement, the wave of young people registering. "Why would the youth want to come to Rome to repent with us?" we wondered. Then we remembered Friedrich Aschoff's interpretation of the blank page from the Wittenberg Bible—that it represented the last verse of the Old Testament, which was about turning the hearts of fathers to their children, and the children to their fathers. "We have fathers *and* children in this meeting!"[6]

---

4 In this case, the traditional English translation of the Italian *piazza* strikes me as odd, because St. Peter's Square is actually round.

5 Their marriage in 2012 made it into the Royal Musings blog: http://royalmusingsblog-spotcom.blogspot.com/2012/07/princely-marriage-cecily-of-salm-salm.html

6 In fact, the German nobility had three generations represented from the Trento meeting forward, and my own family had four generations represented between all the meetings.

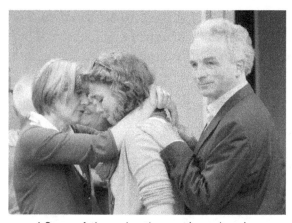

A German father and mother weeping and praying with their daughter. Photo by Ryan and Noleen Thurman. Used with permission.

So we turned our hearts to the youth. And we turned over one night of the meetings to them as well, trusting in their leadership. That night was joyful and even silly—they led the room in singing that ancient hymn: "Father Abraham ... had many sons ... many sons had Father Abraham."

It was also powerful, as Ludwig led worship and the youth blessed the older generation, laying their hands on us and praying for us. And it was poignant, as Cecily took the microphone and tearfully recounted some of the debt of love she owed to the older European generation such as the Marienschwestern.

That youth-full evening in Rome foreshadowed the two remaining meetings, where the younger generation would take an increasingly strong role in leadership.

Use the QR code or visit **https://bit.ly/w17ch18** to explore a map, more pictures, and additional material for this chapter, including the connection between the third Jerusalem temple and the Colosseum (hint: it runs through an arch).

Part IV

The 500th Anniversary,
2016-2017

Chapter 19

500 Days Before, 2016

Concerning Wittenberg, this is what I can share being at that location. It was a moment of direct confrontation for me. On the one hand, the tragedy of the great split that took place in Europe as the Reformation was birthed, but also the sense of what was felt at that time as the light of Christ penetrated the darkness and then feeling the great pain being confronted with Martin Luther's hatred for the Jewish people, whom he had recognized as being Jesus's brethren in his earlier days. My pain was the pain that I felt the Lord experienced as anti-Semitism deeply blemished the face of his church. I was thankful for the repentance that took place during the time that we met.

BENJAMIN BERGER, Messianic Jew, Jerusalem, Israel

It was a spiritual journey bringing together followers of Jesus Christ from different nations and backgrounds—not without challenges and conflict but with heartfelt love toward our Lord Jesus and brotherly love toward one another. There were painful moments where we felt the torn body of our Lord (in front of my eyes I see … the table of the Lord with wine, bread, and the Jewish prayer-shawl in Trento); there were cheerful moments when we felt we are one body, one family, in praying and feasting; there were moments of deep concern for each other when we saw one part of the body suffering (I remember our messianic Jewish brother Richard in Wittenberg lamenting about the "Jewish Pig"); there were tears in moments of confession and repentance where we owned the guilt of our church and forefathers; there were moments of healing embracing God's forgiveness—embracing one another …

For me personally this journey with those many precious moments meant a lot and had an impact in broadening my view for the many-faceted and colorful gems in all the different denominations and congregations.

SISTER DAMIANA LERP † 2021, Marienschwestern
(Evangelical Sisters of Mary–Lutheran), Darmstadt, Germany

When I stepped onto the Wittenberg train platform for the first time in 2010, my heart had been racing. It was racing again in June 2016, even though I had been there several times in the intervening years. For the first time, the Wittenberg 2017 meeting had arrived in Wittenberg.

Amy and I spoke on the first morning to the 120 assembled to pray, to worship, to repent. We once again asked Julia to translate for us. We felt she would not only pass along our words but our heart.

We spoke on grief.

Lament.

Not a popular topic in America, or in the church at large.

> *In Scripture, God does not simply cut out the source of his pain and discard it. He never is described as masking or dulling his own pain. But God also never accepts the pain as normal.*
>
> *Instead, God grieves.*

We then brought forward seven actions of grieving that we learned from Jesus:

1. Refuse all comfort except god's (Matt 5:4)[7]

2. Express your frustration with the powerless church (Matt 17:14–17)

3. Change your location to draw near to pain (John 11)

4. Imagine what is lost (Luke 19:41–46)

5. Fast from food (Mark 2:19–20)

6. Weep (John 16:20–22)

7. Seek companionship ... and also solitude (Mark 14:33–35)

We closed by inviting everyone in the room to spend an hour in silence, asking the Holy Spirit to help them enter into appropriate grief for some aspect of their lives, whether personal or corporate. We gave people permission to leave the room if desired, and left up on the front screen the apostle Paul's beautiful statement about grief:

---

7 Of course, God uses many means to comfort us. What is intended by this action of grieving is to resist our temptation to self-comfort—through entertainment, "comfort food," or other distractions—and also to resist those who offer false or shallow comfort, like Job's friends.

The sorrow of God produces repentance that leads to salvation and leaves no regret, but the world's sorrow produces death. (2 Cor 7:10)

In that hour, Richard Harvey gathered the courage to visit the Judensau.

What is the "Judensau"?

The Wittenberg Judensau, on the wall of the "Mother Church of the Reformation." Photo by Franz Rathmair. Used with permission.

The German word literally means "Jew-pig." Thirty-three of them exist in modern-day Germany, and nowhere else in the world. These medieval stone sculptures depict Jews being profaned by a pig in some way—intended, of course, to insult the Jews by putting them in association with an animal that God has declared unclean for them.

They are terrible.

The one in Wittenberg is the worst of all.

It is on the Stadtkirche, the City Church, the Mother Church of the Reformation.[8]

And Richard sat under it for an hour. And Richard wept.

He had known, of course, about the Wittenberg Judensau—being a Jewish historian who especially studies European anti-Semitism. But he had never seen it.[9] And Richard wept.

And the next day, we wept as he stood before us all and spoke:

> Let's move on to the Judensau.
>
> And of course, the modern term—Sow Jew—if I say that in Germany, will I be arrested, or put on trial? I hope I would.
>
> And I would like this to be put on trial as well.
>
> These are terrible, abusive insults …
>
> And Luther said this: "Here in Wittenberg, on our parish church, there is a sow, carved in stone. Under her, young piglets and Jews lie suckling. Behind

8 The sculpture dates from 1305, so of course it was originally placed there by Roman Catholics—before the Stadtkirche became the first Protestant church.

9 See appendix 7 for the lament that Richard wrote while he sat under the Judensau that day.

the sow stands a rabbi, who lifts the sow's right leg. With his left hand he pulls her rear over himself. He bends down and looks most studiously under her rear at the Talmud inside … as if he wanted to read and see something difficult and special. This is most likely where the Jews got their Shem HaMephoras."[10]

The word "Shem" is "name"; "Mephoras," the "fully pronounced, fully translated" name of God—because of course we do not say the name of God as Jews, we read Yod He Vav He, the tetragrammaton, and we say "Adonai" or "HaShem" because the name of God is so holy for us.

And Luther and the Judensau, they are going to the very heart of what is most sacred to the Jewish people, which is the name of God—

And Luther is saying that it comes out of a pig!

You just can't do this! It's wrong!

It's desecration of the name of God.

And THAT is on the wall of THIS church!

Under the weightiness
of the Spirit of God, we sat.
Some wept silently.
Others sobbed loudly.
We grieved together.
Our grief united us.

Richard Harvey describing his Messianic Jewish reaction to the Judensau. Photo by Franz Rathmair. Used with permission.

And Richard continued.

… and I'm thinking, should it be destroyed? Should it be taken down?

I leave that to you—it's your country, it's your church …

And again, I just pray Lord, that You would take my words and that You would throw out anything that's not of You and that You would speak to our hearts the things that You want us to learn from this.

---

10 Here Richard quotes from Luther's pamphlet *Vom Schem Hamphoras* (1543), the title and theme of which were inscribed above the sculpture after Luther's death (as can be seen in the photograph on p. 132).

This is really horrific; it's so outrageous, obscene, insulting, fear-making—it is something that I PROTEST in the strongest possible terms.

And if there's any way—human, physical, spiritual, whatever—to change it, let's do it.

Years later, I would ask my teenage son John Patrick what, in the whole Wittenberg journey, was the most memorable to him. "Richard Harvey's talk about the Judensau," he replied immediately.

Something was set in motion that day in 2016 that Richard spoke in Wittenberg. Where is it going? The Lord only knows.

Years earlier, Hanna Miley had recounted her first encounter with the Judensau. She told us that in the year 2000, she and George had visited Wittenberg. They had heard about the Judensau. When they reached the Stadt-kirche, they circum-navigated the church, looking for it with a mixture of dread and determination. At the back corner her gaze lifted, and she saw it looming above her. And a fiercely anti-Semitic sculpture with connections through Martin Luther to Hitler's regime confronted a Jewish Holocaust survivor who was working for reconciliation with former Nazis. At that exact moment dark clouds eclipsed the sun, the temperature dropped, a whirlwind churned up dirt and leaves around George and Hanna, and a sudden downpour chased them into the shelter of a nearby restaurant.

Spiritual forces oppose reconciliation.

The ever-changing dinner table combinations made for many fascinating conversations. Here are (left to right) Richard Harvey, Father Peter Hocken, Stefana Restivo, and Julia Torres-who works closely with Pope Francis. Photo by Thomas Cogdell.

God highlighted the spiritual nature of the battle in a similarly remarkable way on the last day of the 2016 meeting. Following a powerful talk about the situation in the German Lutheran church, Father Peter Hocken—a Roman Catholic priest—was fielding questions along with two Lutheran pastors. Father Peter contrasted the churches by saying that the Catholic Church had good solid leadership, but the people were sometimes difficult to lead; whereas, in the German Lutheran Church, there were good laypeople who at times felt their leaders were going astray. He encouraged all members of these two churches to be in prayer for each other.

As he was speaking, a cold wind began to blow through the open windows. The bright blue sky became suddenly dark. Father Peter finished by saying, "I think both are huge spiritual battles. And in both situations, the outcome—well, we don't know how the battle will work out."

At the moment he said that word "battle," a lightning bolt split the darkness outside and a single massive thunderclap shook the room. We were all stunned … except Father Peter, whose wry British sense of humor came through: "Is that a confirmation?" Everyone laughed, certain that God had added his exclamation point onto Father Peter's insight.

Five minutes later, the sky was blue again.

The battle is real.

And worth fighting.

Use the QR code or visit **https://bit.ly/w17ch19** to explore more pictures and additional material for this chapter, including my video of Martin Luther's university building transforming for a day into a house of prayer.

Chapter 20

Death of a Father

The Wittenberg conference drew us deeper into the heart of God as we walked the ancient streets and participated in lively small group discussions, profound lectures, and, a highlight for me, the KISI Kids dramatic musical presentation of Ruth. This beautiful story of reconciliation and faithfulness was a moving and memorable finale to our time together, and many townspeople attended. After a time of joyous celebratory dancing at the end of the production, we all joined in to sing the Aaronic Blessing together. It felt like the heavens opened and we enjoyed a taste of heavenly unity in this city that has witnessed both the glory and the trauma of the Reformation.

MARCIA ZIMMERMANN, Protestant, Ventura, California

Upon arrival in Jerusalem, we reflected on the passing of Monseigneur Peter Hocken, a Roman Catholic priest, part of the Toward Jerusalem Council II (TJCII) initiative for twenty-one years.

We reviewed a clip of 50,000 Catholic charismatics in the Circus Maximus in Rome celebrating the fiftieth year of their movement followed by a clip of Peter hosting a large convocation of Catholic theologians, bishops, etc., as they unpacked the implications of Romans 9–11 and the testimony of the TJCII repentance initiative. Richard Harvey and Marty Waldman presented on behalf of the Messianic Jewish community and, like other panelists, were often interrupted by spontaneous ovations. Peter died just a few days later. It was evident to all that he had completed his obedience to Jesus, graduated gloriously, without regret or unfinished business.

Andy [Zimmermann] represented me at the funeral in Vienna. We viewed video of the ceremony and began to grapple with our deep sense of loss along with a clear signal for generational transfer. We think we have five years to recognize and empower new leadership for what someone at Wittenberg 2017 said was "the most significant work of repentance and restoration in our generation." May God raise up leaders of Peter's quality in the far more diverse Orthodox world. The reemergence of the Messianic Jews destabilizes every foundation in spite of the fact that the Messianic community is itself fragile and easily divided.

JOHN DAWSON, International Director of Youth with a Mission, New Zealand / California USA

Back in 2008, in Herrnhut, Father Peter Hocken promised to visit us in Austin. And he made good on that promise—not once, but four times! We always marveled at his attention. We were a small ministry, incapable of giving him a broad audience. We could make no significant financial contributions to his ministry. Father Peter had nothing to gain from us. He invested in our lives because the Holy Spirit quickened a faith in him on our behalf. That is the love of a spiritual father.

Toward the end of his first visit, Father Peter asked for a private dinner with Amy and me. That evening we spent hours listening to his impressions of the Spirit's movement in our day and hearing stories of his ministry. He told us about two groups especially close to his heart—groups he convened once each year at his house. The first of these groups, "Achana," was composed of older intercessors who prayed into the wounds of Christian history. The other group was the "Maranatha Family"—a fellowship of young adults with a longing for Christ's return.[1]

As the dinner progressed, Amy was wondering which of these two groups Father Peter would invite us to join. We were just past forty—where did that place us? Apparently, we were "old" in Father Peter s eyes, because he did, in fact, invite us to join the Achana group—which we did in 2011.

I will never forget the joy on Father Peter's face as he watched each of his Achana "sheep" cross the threshold of his house in Hainburg, Austria. Every member of this small flock held a special place in his heart.

Father Peter at his 80th birthday party in Hainburg. Photo by Thomas Cogdell.

Being newcomers—and Americans—we wondered how we would fit into the group. We listened carefully, watching and learning. What we observed made a great impression upon us. It was clear that Father Peter held the spiritual discernment and authority of this circle in high regard. It was also clear that the world did not possess a similar esteem for these brothers and sisters. Even within the

---

1 Father Peter had a great love for young people. One of my favorite memories of his ministry in our midst was a fiery blessing on a young man in our community. Father Peter, who was seventy-nine at the time, lifted this man up off the floor, holding him by the waist, swinging him back and forth like a child, as he prayed for the Holy Spirit to fall. The whole time our young friend was laughing with holy laughter.

church, these intercessors were often treated as square pegs for round holes. Their influence was hidden, but Father Peter saw the gifts in each one.

Before coming to Achana, we had broached the topic of Wittenberg 2017 with Father Peter. In the beginning, he was somewhat standoffish. He was especially uncertain about entangling Protestant–Catholic reconciliation with the Jewish question.[2] He also thought a serious repentance initiative required a small number of well-prepared intercessors. To have the more open invitation to the meetings that we envisioned seemed a potential mistake.

Despite this, Father Peter allowed us to share our vision with the Achana group and recruit intercessors for Wittenberg 2017. Marianna Gol joined the team that day. Hans-Peter and Verena Lang, long-standing members of Achana, had already given us their support. In subsequent years, several other members of Achana would attend Wittenberg meetings. But because of his reservations about our approach, Father Peter himself never showed up—until the Rome gathering in 2015.[3]

Actually, I'm not sure he would have come to Rome, except that he already had a meeting set up with Pope Francis. Since we were in town as well, he agreed to join us. We were, of course, absolutely delighted.

> The poor person who was accompanying him tried to talk him out of this plan, but to no avail.

When Father Peter finally arrived at the retreat center several miles outside of Rome, he looked tired. Upon inquiring, we learned that he had taken a train to within a mile and a half of our meeting place but didn't want to wait on the bus. So he walked—an 83-year-old man with luggage. The poor person who was accompanying him tried to talk him out of this plan, but to no avail. Their walk required crossing a busy highway and ended with a long uphill trek on a narrow, winding road.

Father Peter was a bit odd. He was brilliant, to be sure! His memory was uncanny. On his 80th birthday, I heard him go around the room and

---

2 One other couple, who had a long and distinguished history of working in Germany, had also expressed this opinion to us in 2013.

3 Despite his reservations about the initiative, Father Peter threw himself into the task of refining the Principles document that guided the Wittenberg meetings. When Father Peter reviews a document, it is not a casual exercise. Theology is his love language. While he was visiting in Austin, he spent hours weighing the implications of various words and considering possible alternatives.

tell each person in attendance the date, place, and occasion on which he had met them. He had many of the train tables in Europe memorized and would often tell me which side of the train offered the best views. He could cite the Catechism of the Catholic Church by paragraph number. But he could be socially awkward, just like the intercessors around him. He sometimes cut people off in conversation. He was often unaware of the needs, discomforts, or desires of others. Like all of us, he had weaknesses; but in those weaknesses, Christ is made strong.

I will always remember a moment from the first day of the Rome gathering. It was a Sunday, which presented a problem. The Catholics in our midst would want to attend Mass in Rome. However, we couldn't make a Catholic Mass the only option for our group, since this would put our Protestant and Messianic Jewish brethren in the position of attending a service where they could not partake of the Eucharist.[4] How could we worship together?

Our leadership team turned this problem over to the ten clergy in attendance. Their solution was brilliant. We would tour the Catacombs in the morning, viewing our common heritage in the saints and martyrs of the early church. The tour would end with a service in a chapel above the Catacombs, where we would wash one another's feet—sharing perhaps the only sacred symbol instituted by Jesus that has *not* become a point of division. The clergy would be the ones doing the foot-washing, as an act of repentance for the all-too-common clerical abuse of the laity. Then we would have the afternoon off, so that Catholics could attend Mass at the parish of their choosing.

When the clergy knelt to wash our feet, the presence of the Holy Spirit became powerfully evident. There was joy and awe; there was weeping, even wailing. Priests, pastors, and bishops, many of them over seventy years old, barefoot on the stone floor, caring for the flock—what grace and humility!

When they had washed the feet of the laity, the clergy began to attend to each other.

---

4 In the Trento meeting, we had placed a table with bread and wine in the center each day, as a reminder not of what we were celebrating in common, but of what we could *not* share together, and were thus grieving—namely, that this act given by Jesus for the unity of the church had become instead a point of division.

Father Peter washing Henning's feet above the Catacombs. Photo by Thomas Cogdell.

And Father Peter knelt to wash the feet of Pastor Henning Dobers.

Here was an elderly father blessing a younger, stronger generation.

An Englishman serving a German. A Roman Catholic priest who had served as chaplain to the papal household washing the feet of a Lutheran pastor.

And he did it with such care, very aware of the import of his actions, taking the time to speak words of blessing to Henning.

In turn, Henning washed Father Peter's feet. Beautiful!

All this was done above the tombs of the early church—clergy and laity buried together. Many had given their lives for the gospel, so that we could be here centuries later, seeking reconciliation with each other.

Father Peter addresses our 2016 gathering in Wittenberg. Photo by Franz Rathmair. Used with permission.

Later that week, Father Peter gave a short but important talk in the cloister of St. John Lateran, the cathedral of Rome. The essence of his talk was this: "Roman Catholics can *celebrate* Martin Luther and the 500th anniversary." This was a surprise for us! We were focused on grieving, and Father Peter was talking about celebrating. He would expound on this topic in a profound way the following year in Wittenberg, speaking of the surprises of the Holy Spirit.

Here are some excerpts from his talk given in Wittenberg in 2016.

Martin Luther was a surprise of the Holy Spirit. His three criteria for reform—Christus Solus, Fides Sola,[5] and Sola Scriptura—all came from the Holy Spirit. The modern renewal of the Catholic Church has come as these

5 Father Peter qualified this with "in the sense of fiducia."

three criteria have begun to be accepted. This is why Roman Catholics can, in integrity, celebrate the 500th anniversary of the Reformation.

Verena Lang had taught us to *honor* Martin Luther as a prophet to her church. Now Father Peter was teaching us to *celebrate* Luther's prophetic words—the message that deeply challenged his own Roman Catholic Church for centuries!

Reconciliation is NOT reconstruction! There is a new work of the Holy Spirit in our day. Wittenberg 2017 is one of the surprises of the Holy Spirit. The Holy Spirit is creative, never repeating what was done before. A reconciled body in unity will be a creative work of the Holy Spirit.[6]

This talk in 2016 was joyful and electrifying! Everyone in attendance looked forward to what this vibrant, Spirit-filled scholar would bring to our final gathering.

But Father Peter Hocken did not attend the final Wittenberg 2017 meeting.

At least, not in his earthly body.

The week before he died, Father Peter was in good health, visiting Rome again. He had come with tens of thousands of others in May 2017 to celebrate the golden jubilee of the Catholic Charismatic Renewal. He had come to teach.

On June 1, Father Peter participated in a panel discussion of distinguished experts, including Father Raniero Cantalamessa and Pentecostal pastor Vinson Synan.[7] The topic was the Catholic Charismatic Renewal and the wider worldwide charismatic and Pentecostal movements of the twentieth century.[8]

---

6 The foreword is excerpted from this teaching, and contains a QR code link to a recording of the full talk.

7 Pope Francis had courageously insisted this celebration of the Holy Spirit must not be just a Catholic event—because the Pentecostal and charismatic outpourings had touched all parts of the body of Christ. For the official Vatican press release about this event, see https://press.vatican.va/content/salastampa/en/bollettino/pubblico/2017/06/03/170603g.html.

8 The study of the Pentecostal and charismatic movements was one of Father Peter's passions. In fact, he served as executive director of the Society for Pentecostal Studies for almost a decade—a Catholic priest chosen to lead a Protestant organization! Much of his writing and teaching, which can be found at https://www.peterhocken.org/, focuses on or at least touches the Pentecostal and charismatic movements of the twentieth century.

The next day, June 2, Father Peter led a panel discussion on the topic of Messianic Jews and their witness to the church. For many years, Father Peter had served as an advocate and bridge builder for the emerging Messianic movement. Finally, this discussion was coming into the open before a wide audience that included leaders within the Vatican. Johannes Fichtenbauer and Richard Harvey, who had spoken at our Trento meeting, were on the panel along with Rabbi Marty Waldman from Texas. The event was packed.[9]

The large video screen captures the typical secret smile of Father Peter (far left), showing the joy that he felt at the Rome Jubilee as Father Raniero Cantalamessa addresses the gathering. Photo by Ryan and Noleen Thurman. Used with permission.

On June 3, Father Peter sat with Pope Francis on the main stage for the Vigil of Pentecost. George and Hanna Miley, Hans-Peter and Verena Lang, and Ryan Thurman were also on the stage as representatives of Wittenberg 2017. The Circus Maximus was filled with tens of thousands of Spirit-filled believers from around the world.

These three days represented the culmination of Father Peter's life work. After they were over, he was asked what he was going to do next. Eyes twinkling, Father Peter quoted the Song of Simeon:

Now dismiss Thy servant, O Lord, in peace, according to Thy word: For mine own eyes hath seen thy salvation, Which Thou hast prepared in the sight of all the peoples, a light to reveal Thee to the nations and the glory of Thy people Israel. (Traditional wording of the Nunc Dimittis, Luke 2:29–32)

On June 5, he returned to Herrnhut.

On June 10, 2017—Father Peter died.

News of his death spread quickly around the world. People from many nations, denominations, and all ranks of life flocked to Hainburg for his funeral. I am sure local residents were shocked that day to find streets blocked by a colorful crowd of young people singing, Jews praying the Kaddish, and vested clergy processing with the coffin of the odd old priest who lived among them. They must have wondered—"Who was this man?"

---

9 I know this even though I wasn't there, because Phillip and Caroline Owens were, and they reported being prevented from entering because the auditorium had reached capacity.

Not everyone who labors at a task given by the Lord receives this kind of ending. Few see the culmination of their life's work as Father Peter did in Rome. But you, reader, you should know that God sees. He is the best of fathers. He sees the treasure hidden in every soul. He remembers every act of faith, whether it is performed in public or private. And he is the one who will surely make that glory visible throughout eternity.

Use the QR code or visit https://bit.ly/w17ch20 to explore more pictures and additional material for this chapter, including an audio recording of the lightning bolt and thunderclap that sealed Father Peter's words in Wittenberg.

Chapter 21

Death of a Mother

My wife and I went to the next-to-last meeting, which was in Wittenberg, Germany. It was a pleasant trip, full of rich memories, but my choicest memories were from the plenary sessions. I heard Dr. Richard Harvey's impassioned talk about the Judensau on Luther's church, in which he announced that he could never worship God in that church; and also Father Peter Hocken's comment that was followed by loud thunder from the thunderstorm in progress at the time. Hocken got an impish grin on his face and said that the thunder showed God's approval of his words.

JOHN R. COGDELL (my father), Anglican, McGregor, Texas USA

I want to end this overview of the June [2016] gathering by telling you some of the things that were brought home to me. I realized that I can't enter well into what I'll call "identificational repentance" when really I'm indifferent; and I'm indifferent when things are distant from me—distant in history or distant in the present, geographically or emotionally. In particular, being in the midst of those who were definitely not indifferent (and Europeans seem to have so much a better sense of history than many of us Americans; they're more connected), I felt the pain of not being able to respond as fully as I'd have liked. The process of praying prayers of identificational repentance is both humbling and necessarily cleansing—looking at the sin of another or a grievous event of history, I felt that my eyes needed to be purified so that I could look with care rather than point the finger.

ANN COGDELL † 2017 (my mother),
Anglican, heaven (before that, McGregor, Texas)

My mother's hidden glory was also revealed in her burial one month after Father Peter's. Hers, however, was a very different glory than his.

Perhaps the death of Ann Safford Cogdell on the last day of July 2017 was also a surprise of the Holy Spirit. It was certainly unexpected. Looking back, though, we could see how the Lord had allowed us to prepare for what we didn't know was coming. And Wittenberg 2017 played a part.

On the last day of the 2016 meeting, we had announced three activities for the 500 Days leading up to the 500th anniversary: fasting, prayer, and study. I felt as a leader I should set an example. So for the "study" portion, I took on the ambitious project of creating one meme about reconciliation every day, to post to Facebook and Instagram. I called it, "Door of the Day"—because each picture had a door or opening in it, and each quotation was a "door opening" into reconciliation and healing.[1]

500 Door of the Day postings. One per day, for 500 straight days.

Looking back, I don't know how I pulled this off. It had to have been the grace of God. There were times when I was driving to work, and suddenly realized—I haven't posted my door yet! I would pull off at a Starbucks to hastily post that day's door. I think I only missed a couple of days, out of the entire 500—and those I made up quickly. So I ended up with a library of 500 reconciliation memes.

As I mentioned in chapter 8, I'm an artist wannabe. I saw my chance in early 2017 and approached the arts pastor at Hope Chapel.[2] I proposed a "Door of the Day" exhibit, complete with actual doors hung up on the church walls. He went for it. We decided to make it collaborative—inviting seven people to choose a few memes each and then write short descriptions of why they chose the ones they did.

> ... she was an artist in the depths of her soul.

I wanted the first curator to be ... my mother.

My mom was a true artist. Not just that she was an Oberlin-trained concert pianist ... she was an artist in the depths of her soul. Everything was art—each room of her house, each meal, each tag on each Christmas present, each carefully considered comment in a discussion. I knew that Mom would take the assignment seriously, and that she would likely surprise me with her choices.

---

1 See The 500 Days/Door of the Day on the Wittenberg 2017 website (http://www.wittenberg2017.us/door-of-the-day.html).

2 David Taylor had long since moved on, and the current pastor was my friend Brett Hart.

My mother, Ann, and my father, John, in the kitchen of their "31st Street House" in Austin, where they welcomed so many with the art of hospitality. Photo by Thomas Cogdell.

The exhibit was supposed to open in early June. But it was postponed because the previous exhibit had not been up long enough. Then it was postponed again. When the opening Sunday finally arrived, I was asked to give a short introduction. I invited all seven curators to come, and most did—including my mom, who drove down to Austin with my dad from their home on a farm.

Hope Chapel was in the midst of a sermon series on the Ten Commandments. The sermon for that Sunday was on the Fourth Commandment—"Honor your father and mother … that it may go well with you in the land the LORD is giving you" (Deut 5:16). Having learned about the importance of honoring parents from George Miley, and also from Friedrich Aschoff, I decided to take a risk.

I finished the introduction to the exhibit, then I turned in the pulpit to my mother and asked her to stand. "Mom, I want you to know, if there is anything of beauty in all of this—it came from you." By "this" I meant not just the artwork on the wall, but all of the memes, all of Wittenberg 2017, indeed all of my life of reconciliation. I think she understood. Perhaps the other worshippers in attendance did as well, because they stood and applauded her. She told me afterward that my words had surprised her.

The date was July 23, 2017.

The next Saturday Mom and Dad again made the two-hour drive down, this time for a retreat at our ministry center. The topic, chosen to help us prepare for the final Wittenberg gathering later that year, was Godly Love. For this July retreat, we focused on Paul's amazing discourse in his first letter to the Corinthians. "If I have the gift of prophecy, and can understand all mysteries and all knowledge, and if I have great faith that can move mountains, but I do not live a life of love … I'm nothing."[3]

During the group discussion, my mother made a few comments. One of them captured the essence of Ann Cogdell:

What strikes me is how much God cares about who we are. Because it's love that builds us up, and so it seems like God is after what kind of person we become.

So an implication would be, that for beauty to come forth, love has to be present.

When I said goodbye to her afterward, she told me that she felt that she needed to grow more in love. Then we embraced each other. I didn't know that this would be our last hug and our final conversation.

On the drive back to the farm, my dad turned to her. My father is an engineer—and all that that implies! He is not given to displays of physical affection or direct expressions of emotion. But that day, inspired by Paul's words, and certainly guided by the Holy Spirit, he said to her something he later told me he hadn't said in years: "Ann, I loved you the day I married you, and I love you just as much today."

The date was July 29, 2017.

Mom's day was not done when she arrived back at the farm. She practiced her piano late into that Saturday night. Why did she do this? She was certainly tired from the long day of driving.

Well, she had broken her arm a few months earlier, and the doctor's diagnosis was uncertain as to whether she would ever play piano again.

But the piano was woven into my mother's soul. She did her physical therapy diligently and worked hard after her cast came off. That Sunday, the next day,

Mom invites one of her grandchildren to sign the cast on her broken arm. Photo by Rebekah/Sarah Brydon. Used with permission.

she was signed up to play in church for the first time since the accident. So she felt the need to practice, since she hadn't played for other people

---

3 1 Cor 13:2, ellipsis added for emphasis. Dear reader, we lose a treasure by relegating 1 Corinthians 13 to weddings only! Rightly would the church daily live in this passage, take it to heart, learn from it, and be transformed.

for many months. Her Steinway grand piano completely filled a small shed on the farm, leaving room only for a dehumidifier to keep the valuable instrument in tune. As she tried different chord progressions in Luther's hymn "A Mighty Fortress Is Our God," there was something she did not know. She was being recorded.

Her grandson Jonathan, who lived in another house on the farm, had long wanted to have a video of his "Grannie Annie" practicing the piano. As he heard her that night, he first thought, "Not now, I can do this any time." But a more urgent thought came: "I should record her *now*." So he crept out with his camera, pointed it at the window that was spilling light into the darkness, set the focus on his grandmother as she swayed back and forth on the piano bench, and pressed the record button.

The next day was Sunday, July 30, 2017.

> But a more urgent thought came: "I should record her *now*."

Mom sat at the piano bench of Christ Church Anglican in Waco and accompanied the hymns. Then she went to sit down next to my dad. The worshippers started proceeding forward for communion. Before the usher reached their pew, Mom turned and said, "John, I'm seeing double … I think I am having a stroke." She slumped down next to him. An ambulance was called and she was rushed to the hospital. After a long night lying comatose, surrounded by the love of her family, she drew her last breath when dawn broke.

The date was July 31, 2017.

She died at dawn and was buried at sunset. Her body rested in a simple pine coffin handmade by my dad in preparation for his own future funeral—yes, one of her first actions in eternity was to borrow her husband's casket.

Father Lee, her Anglican priest, made the sign of the cross. The grandchildren began to sing, "One glad morning, when this life is over … I'll fly away …" We all pitched in to fill the grave, the first in the simple cemetery on their family farm. My

The funeral service in the living room of my parents' farm house in McGregor, Texas.
Photo by Christina Cogdell.
Used with permission.

young daughter was weeping inconsolably, which blended with the singing voices as the shoveling of earth continued into the deepening dusk.

For beauty to come forth, love has to be present.

And in my mind the death of my mother came to be paired with the death of Father Peter. The death of a spiritual father had been closely followed by the death of an actual mother. God honored Father Peter by allowing him to see the culmination of his earthly ministry. God honored my mother by making her death and burial a day of astonishing beauty—"the most beautiful day of my life," in the words of one of my sisters.

For beauty to come forth, love has to be present.

In the end, then, neither Father Peter nor Ann Cogdell attended the final Wittenberg gathering—though I am sure that they were both in the "cloud of witnesses" watching from the gallery of heaven. Perhaps they sat together, comparing memories of their remarkable deaths and burials, and enjoying all that God was doing.

They saw that love was present at the 500th anniversary of the Protestant Reformation.

And they saw that beauty came forth.

Use the QR code or visit **https://bit.ly/w17ch21** to explore more pictures and additional material for this chapter, including the video we showed at my mother's memorial service, which includes her last recorded words about love and beauty, as well as the video shot by her nephew the night before her stroke.

Chapter 22

Searching for Anabaptists

Thank you for your prayers and for the birthday greetings that many people sent me. June was a very blessed month. The meeting in Wittenberg [2016] was excellent, wonderfully led in a graced way by Thomas and Amy Cogdell. My teaching, which underwent considerable revision during the meeting, will be available on websites soon.

FATHER PETER HOCKEN, † Roman Catholic, Hainburg, Austria

Having received a personal invitation from Hans-Peter Lang (Austria) to attend this gathering in Wittenberg, we were super excited. We met in Wittenberg jointly, with a delegation of Anabaptists from the USA, Switzerland, and Germany—a team that has been reaching out to other movements in the body of Christ for healing and reconciliation.

The highlight of this gathering was meeting with Thomas and Amy Cogdell, from Texas, who welcomed us with open arms. We were deeply impressed with their leadership, which they conducted with great humility and with much grace. It was amazing to behold the various movements in the body of Christ as they joined hands in unity, humility, and forgiveness.

BEN GIROD SR. and BENJAMIN GIROD JR., Amish,
Anabaptist Connections, Libby, Montana

"If there isn't repentance regarding the Radical Reformation, we shouldn't bother to have the meeting."

Johannes Fichtenbauer, the archdeacon of the Diocese of Vienna, expressed this strong opinion to the leadership team as we entered into planning for the final gathering in 2017. Our most important question was this:

What would be our focus for repentance?

Throughout the preceding five years, the Langs had led us on a journey of repentance. One of the principles we operated under was, "Repent for your own tradition ... honor the other traditions." This is opposite of the normal tendency, to blindly honor our own tradition while "repenting" only for the sins and perceived weaknesses of the others. So in every meeting, as we knelt together in humility before the Lord, we were led into repentance by the appropriate offending party. Anti-Semitism was acknowledged by representatives of gentile Christian traditions … Verena Lang, a Catholic, brought to light the Catholic refusal of Martin Luther's prophetic message … bishops and priests confessed the misplaced priorities of wealth and edifice-building … and German Lutheran pastors mourned the current waywardness of their church.

What remained?

In this respect, Father Peter left us a gift before he died.

"We can't forget the Radical Reformation," he had forcefully told both me and Verena Lang, separately, on several occasions.

In addition to Johannes and Father Peter, one other significant leader affirmed the importance of addressing the Radical Reformation during the 2017 gathering.

The TJCII prayer journey in Prague, with John Dawson (*far right*). I am two rows above him, joined by many other Wittenberg 2017 participants who were also on this pilgrimage. Photo by Thomas Cogdell.

John Dawson currently serves as the international director of YWAM, but I had been profoundly influenced by him decades earlier. In 1998, I had read his book *Healing America's Wounds*, which recounted stories of identificational repentance toward Native Americans and African

Americans in the United States.[1] I had felt as if a new world opened up to me. Then, in 2015, I found myself in Prague for a prayer journey that John Dawson helped to lead.

On the first day I just observed him from a distance with the kind of awe reserved for a hero that you never imagined you would actually meet.

The second day, I found myself walking next to John as our group made its way through the narrow streets of Prague. It was now or never. I summoned up all my courage to speak, and mentioned to him that I was working on a reconciliation initiative regarding the upcoming 500th anniversary of the Protestant Reformation. I asked if I could have some time to seek his counsel. He kindly and earnestly replied that he had been hoping to talk about this with me as well. I tried not to show too much of the delight I felt in that moment, but I called Amy later to tell her, "I'm going to get to tell John Dawson about Wittenberg!"

We had dinner together that evening, and I recounted the outlines of the story I have told in the first part of this book. He listened carefully, then suggested we meet again over breakfast.

The next morning, John first asked, "So, who is involved?" When I mentioned Sister Joela and the Marienschwestern, he seemed relieved— "Good, then the anointing of God will be on this initiative." He immediately began to brainstorm strategic ideas about the gathering in 2017. My frantic note-taking ended with his final thought, "And, of course, we can't forget the Radical Reformation. That must be addressed."

There it was again … the Radical Reformation!

John Dawson. Father Peter. Johannes Fichtenbauer.

To have all three of these very different leaders point in the same direction gave a strong sense that it was the Lord who was communicating this to us.

So, you may be asking, what *is* the Radical Reformation?

I had the same question, because I knew very little of this part of church history. Here is a summary of what I learned.

Around the time of the Reformation, groups began to form who believed

---

1 If you are not familiar with identificational repentance, you may want to reread the Midword, which was written by John Dawson. Appendix 5 also contains a theological introduction to this concept.

that Luther wasn't going far enough by separating only from the institutional church in Rome—because the Lutherans remained intertwined with the institution of the state. This was a matter of expediency for Luther: it was the princes in Germany who held off the political and military power of the Vatican, preserving his freedom and in fact his very life. But the "Radical Reformers" clung closely to Jesus's teachings to detach from political governments and refuse all acts of violence. They sought to *live out* the Sermon on the Mount.

The Radical Reformers did not practice infant baptism common, which was to all Christian traditions at that time. They believed that it was not a Scriptural baptism if the individual had no understanding or choice in the act. They came to be known as "Anabaptists," meaning "another baptism"— referring to being baptized again as an adult.[2]

While the Protestants and Catholics of those days disagreed about many things, in this they were united—their hatred of the Anabaptists. Rome persecuted and killed the Anabaptists. Lutherans and Calvinists persecuted and killed the Anabaptists. In the end, the few survivors mostly fled Europe. Current American communities such as the Amish, Mennonites, and Hutterites trace their spiritual and often physical ancestry back to the Anabaptist refugees from centuries before.[3]

> While the Protestants and Catholics of those days disagreed about many things, in this they were united–their hatred of the Anabaptists.

This was the Radical Reformation.

Faced with this history, our leadership team made the decision: in the 2017 gathering, the Catholics and Protestants would jointly repent to the Anabaptists.

The problem was ... none of us knew any Anabaptists!

Repentance must be received. What Anabaptists would receive this repentance? Many of our leadership meetings over the 500 days were spent on this topic.

---

2 Since they consider that adult baptism is not "another" baptism, but actually the first valid baptism, some who are called Anabaptists prefer not to go by that name.
3 Even though their numbers were few and they were persecuted, Anabaptists are considered to have had a profound influence on the development of the principle of religious freedom in Western civilization.

We did have two participants from previous meetings who had Anabaptist backgrounds: Franz Rathmair and Jill Margheim-Baggerman. Franz was taking an increasingly active role in the Wittenberg 2017 initiative, and he had done some research into Anabaptist persecution in his hometown of Steyr, Austria. Jill was from Hope Chapel in Austin, and she and her husband Tim were a delightful young couple who had come to the Rome meeting.

Hans-Peter and Verena uncovered the name of Wolfgang Krauss, an Anabaptist historian based in Augsburg. The Langs made contact with him, but there didn't seem to be much interest on his side in coming to the meeting.

I also remembered a small Anabaptist thread that I could begin pulling. On December 7, 2015, a couple had visited us in Texas from the Bruderhof, a community based in upstate New York. Twelve of us sat around a large table and heard from them about the spiritual heritage of the Bruderhof. Our hearts bonded with theirs that night over a shared desire for the unity of the body of Christ. The Bruderhof had begun in the 1920s in Germany, and (I now remembered a year later) they considered themselves to be ... Anabaptists!

Map of the Houston Zoo.
The "You Are Here" sign in the center was almost precisely where I was during my call with Martin Johnson of the Bruderhof.
Photo by Thomas Cogdell

In the spring of 2017, that couple put me in contact with one of the Bruderhof elders, Martin Johnson. I will never forget the unusual setting for our first phone call together. Amy and I were on our way to Germany for a planning meeting. We decided to drive down as a family to Houston one day early, to give ourselves some extra time before our flight ... and to be able to visit the zoo. Cogdells like zoos!

So that was where I placed this important call to Martin Johnson of the Bruderhof. While my family was enjoying lions and tigers and bears (oh my!) ... I was engrossed in our conversation. I held my cell phone close to my ear while walking on the zoo's spacious and lovely paths, surrounded by tourists with cameras and small children asleep in strollers.

Our hour-long discussion was occasionally interrupted by the scream of some nearby beast. I explained Wittenberg 2017, our themes of repentance, and our Historical Conclusions.[4] Martin asked several questions that showed he was listening carefully. He clearly understood both the need for and the importance of repentance toward the Anabaptists. At the same time, he made it clear to me that he felt the Anabaptists would also need to repent—of withdrawing into a defensive posture, rather than being the prophetic witness that the world needed them to be.

Martin suggested that the path forward would be for the Langs to contact Chris Zimmerman. Chris and his wife, Bea, were leading a new Bruderhof community in Germany. And in fact, a few months later, the Langs received the welcome word that the Zimmermans would be coming to Wittenberg. This proved to be a connection that would have far-reaching consequences.

Just a few months before the gathering, we again saw the intentionality of the Father in answering his Son's prayer. Somehow, Mennonites from Pennsylvania heard about our gathering and notified us that they were bringing a delegation. We would come to deeply love Keith Blank, Lloyd Hoover, and the others in this group.

In turn, they reached out and invited some Amish from Idaho. And Ben Shirod, a leader in that community, would come as well and bring his son.

And the Langs had received word back from Wolfgang Krauss—he, too, would come, to give a talk on the history of Anabaptist persecution.

When we heard this, we were delighted.

The Anabaptists were coming!

 Use the QR code or visit **https://bit.ly/w17ch22** to explore more pictures and additional material for this chapter, including a description of the "red line" of Franziskus's teachings.

---

4 See appendix 2, Historical Conclusions about the Reformation.

A Prayer Meeting Occasionally Interrupted by Teachings

The week of October 31, 2017, will always be remembered as profoundly significant. Two days prior to traveling to Wittenberg, I had the privilege of being in Israel to witness the events surrounding the 100th anniversary of the Battle of Beersheba, considered by modern Israelis as the catalyst event leading to the creation of the Jewish state. October 31, 2017, also marked 100 years since the signing of the Balfour Declaration. We then joined intercessors in Wittenberg for the 500th anniversary of the Reformation, where representatives from church streams came together to offer and receive forgiveness, with a deep spirit of humility over the wounds inflicted to the body of Christ. God poured out his healing grace, as we dealt with the original separation between Jews and Gentiles that occurred in the days of the early church, during the Reformation, and to the present day. In Wittenberg, we experienced a touch of the unity Jesus prayed for in John 17.

ANDY ZIMMERMANN, Protestant, Toward Jerusalem Council II
(TJCII) Leadership Council, Ventura, California USA

The day we arrived in Wittenberg from Berlin, we attended the opening gathering of Wittenberg 2017. During this gathering, everyone attending joined in worship together to our King, in what seemed like every language and stream of the body of Christ. I had never heard so many different voices praising God in one room before, and what a beautiful sound it was. Hearing and observing this brought me to tears, gave me a hope and a peace, and greatly encouraged me for what is to come. In those moments, I caught a glimpse of what the Father is doing and the number of lives he is changing.

ABIGAIL TRANTHAM COGDELL, Hope Chapel (Protestant /
nondenominational), Austin, Texas USA

John 17.
For Jesus to have prayed for the church of our day is remarkable.

For Jesus's prayer to have been remembered is remarkable.

For Jesus's remembered prayer to have been recorded is remarkable.

And for the record of Jesus's prayer to have been preserved and passed down through the ages is ... well, remarkable. So what word should be used to describe the contents of that prayer?

"Remarkable" is far too weak a word. "Unbelievable" and "astonishing" fall short as well.[1]

Jesus prays that the church, those who believe in Jesus through the disciples' message, "will be brought to *complete unity* ... that they will be one *as we are one*" (John 17:23, 22; emphasis added).

That our relationships—human to human, group to group, community to community—could look and feel like the relationship between the First Person of the Trinity and the Second Person of the Trinity ... if Jesus had not opened the door to this possibility, and John had not listened and recorded—well, who could have conceived of it?

But he did open that door. And so we can walk through with confidence.

We can pray John 17 with Jesus.

Praying John 17 together was part of our original vision from the year 2000. In my mind's eye, I always saw a day-and-night prayer room in Wittenberg. A Protestant team handing off to a Catholic team, handing off to a German team, handing off to an American team, handing off to a single guitarist, handing off to a full worship ensemble, hour after hour, day after day.

The leadership council was not so sure! And of course, we were committed to preserving the unity of the council. This could not be a decision that I made unilaterally.

The primary challenge was to communicate the picture I had in my mind. Most of the wonderful older believers on the council—the Langs, the Mileys, Franziskus—had never experienced a day-and-night prayer room. They only had experienced continual prayer during a conference

---

1 "Overlooked" and "ignored" come to mind ... but that is another book altogether.

as a group of intercessors in a separate nearby location, praying *for* the meeting's success. So it was understandably difficult to grasp prayer as an integral part of the program.

I finally was able to communicate my intention with this statement:

> *Wittenberg will not be a conference of teachings with some prayer on the side; instead, it will be a prayer meeting occasionally interrupted by teachings.*

A prayer meeting occasionally interrupted by teachings.

The Germanic peoples love teachings … they really love teachings. For them to consider the possibility that the teaching would not be the culmination point, but simply a guidepost to prayer—now, this was a new idea!

They got it.

We decided that during the day, we would take that description literally. The prayer teams would not be off in a separate room, but be on stage. They would start as early as the Stadthaus[2] would allow, which was 8:00 AM. In between speakers, they would come back up to lead us in a prayerful response to each session, responding to what that speaker had brought forth.

> It is the night watch that makes continuous prayer so difficult.

And after the last speaker, the teams would continue praying and worshipping until 10:00 PM, when we had to vacate the building.

What about 10 PM to 8 AM? What about the all-important night watch?

It is the night watch that makes continuous prayer so difficult. Yet, paradoxically, it is the night watch that makes continuous prayer so powerful and rewarding. I will never forget my first night watch, which was over the turn of the century, the last night of 1999 and the first morning of 2000. While the rest of America was worrying about computer systems failing, we were worshipping God in the new millennium. Through the

---

2 The meeting rooms for the 2017 gathering included the Best Western Melanchthonsaal, which had been reserved in 2010, and the Leucorea, which Julia and I visited then as well. However, our main sessions took place in the Wittenberg Stadthaus. The Stadthaus was a lovely modern conference center that had been built since 2010, specifically in preparation for the 500th anniversary. It was the only room that could hold the 400+ attendees that our initiative had grown to. Click the QR code at the end of the chapter to learn more about the rooms and the dates of the final meeting.

years, I saw that God rewards in a special way those who labor in night prayer. Sometimes it is difficult, and so often the eyelids desperately want to close—and yet, then the presence of God draws near, and time becomes irrelevant in the company of the Almighty Lover of mankind.

During our visit to Wittenberg in 2016, we had met an exceptional woman. Frau Birgitte Neumeister was the pastor of Hoffnung Kirche, a Baptist church in Wittenberg. Pastor Neumeister opened up the basement of her church for our night watch. It was perfect! Newly remodeled and within easy walking distance of the Stadthaus. We had our location for the night watch, and we could easily make a worship procession from there to the Stadthaus in the morning, and back in the late evening.

And so the Lord provided a way for Wittenberg 2017 to be a prayer meeting occasionally interrupted by teachings. Wonderful prayer teams volunteered from around Europe and the United States—Catholic, Protestant, Messianic Jewish; young and old; free-flowing and liturgical— all sharing love for Jesus and for his people. And it was absolutely beautiful.

> I retraced my steps and approached cautiously—it can be dangerous to surprise someone in their sleep.

One morning, I set my alarm for 3:00 AM. It was important for me, as a leader, to show up at the night watch, even though I had responsibilities all through the day.

As I exited into the darkness, I shivered and wrapped my leather jacket around myself, thankful for its warmth. Suddenly, I saw a vagrant under a nearby staircase. *Unusual to see a homeless person in Germany*, I thought to myself, as I hurried past toward the prayer room. With every step I took, my conscience pricked me more and more. How could I go pray, without helping this person? I retraced my steps and approached cautiously—it can be dangerous to surprise someone in their sleep. As I bent over, I saw that this was a man, grizzled and weary with slumber. His blanket was a patchwork of rags and clothes, draped over as much of his body as possible.

I removed my jacket and used it to cover his torso, then backed away. He stirred in his sleep, and his arm grabbed part of my jacket—now his—and pulled it tighter around his body, to keep in the warmth. I melted away into the street, satisfied but now a wee bit chilly! My five-minute walk was brisk.

When I opened the door to the prayer room, the light and warmth and music flooded out. I was surprised to see that the room was full. I had to squeeze through to find a place in the corner where I could lay down my Bible and pace a few steps in each direction.

Alexander Dietsche and Brother Pietro had joined together to lead us, singing out spontaneous, new songs in the middle of the night. "Awake harp and lyre … I will awaken the dawn!" (Ps 57:8).

Rupert from Vienna plays the saxophone during the night watch. Photo by Ryan and Noleen Thurman. Used with permission.

As I joined in, all sleepiness vanished, and time became less relevant. They were succeeded by a team from Austin that included my youngest son, John Patrick, who was fourteen at the time but already very gifted on guitar. A year or so later, I asked him what his favorite moment was during that final Wittenberg gathering. "Oh, playing on Michel's team during the night watch, for sure!" Would you suspect that a young teenager would be interested in prayer at 5:00 AM? The Holy Spirit has many surprises …

I stumbled back to bed at six, and was up again at seven for breakfast, a leadership meeting, and then the trek to the Stadthaus. When I entered, once again I was astounded at how many were there early, worshipping and dancing, praying and lifting up their hands. The team from Vienna was leading—saxophone, drums, guitars, vocals, all honed through hours of solitary prayer in the prayer room. Now they were in a large meeting hall, with expert sound engineers and eager participants—what a joy that must have been for them! As their time drew to an end, Phillip Owens from the Christ the Reconciler community came up on the stage and joined in on backup guitar—a beautifully humble and gentle transition into his time of leading worship. He encouraged the Vienna team to stay on and play with him for the morning worship, and my oldest son Noah also joined in. And it was as if they had played together for years! Their impromptu combined worship session—ah, the world is not worthy of such beauty.[3]

---

3 That morning became all the more poignant in 2019, when we learned that Gunter, the drummer from Vienna, had been killed in a farm accident. I will always remember him giving all of his heart to the Lord as he drummed in unison with a worship team that he had never played with before. Perhaps that team will have a reunion in heaven, that Gunter is even now preparing for!

My friend Phillip Owens (center) with my son Noah (right), leading worship and prayer together with Hanna Platzer from the Lüdenscheid community. Photo by Ryan and Noleen Thurman. Used with permission.

"A prayer meeting occasionally interrupted by teachings"—it worked! By the time a speaker took the stage, there was such a spirit of love and receptivity in the room. And when he or she finished, the team that followed would sensitively adjust to the themes of the talk and the corresponding mood in the room, giving an unhurried chance for us to respond in prayer and worship.

These are all human observations, felt and seen.

How did heaven receive it?

What was the response of the angels, who fall down whenever the living creatures cry out, "Holy, holy, holy"?

Were our prayers like incense in the awesome bowls before the throne of God, wafting up to bring pleasure to the Almighty?

And when Messianic Jews joined together with Protestant, Catholic, and Eastern Orthodox believers from around the world to lift up the same prayer that his Son had prayed—for unity—was the Father's heart moved?

Eternity will tell …

Use the QR code or visit **https://bit.ly/w17ch23** to explore more pictures and additional material for this chapter, including how German chancellor Angela Merkel played a role in the timing of our conference.

Chapter 24

The Joy of Repentance

When I offered to serve in whatever way might be helpful at Wittenberg 2017, I had no idea how God would touch me through this time with wonderful brothers and sisters in Christ like the two of you [the Mileys]. You are gems shining brightly with the Lord's glory. Thank you! Thank you! Thank you! I was inspired, stirred, torn apart (with the depth of the brokenness in the Body), filled with hope, and blessed beyond description.

As I fly across the Atlantic, my heart is full, my mind is processing, and my spirit is at peace. This was truly an encounter with God and with his saints. Bless you, Hanna and George!

KEITH BLANK, bishop, Lancaster Mennonite Conference
(Anabaptist), Lancaster, Pennsylvania USA

This was a kingdom of heaven conference, filled with seasoned believers who reflected Yeshua's light and glory. What a joy to celebrate Shabbat in Germany with Holy Spirit–filled Catholic priests and Lutheran pastors plus Anabaptists, who were once slaughtered by the former and all of whom at that time despised the likes of me! Because of a move of the Spirit, Shabbat was a picture of heaven—Jew and Gentile one in Messiah! No one was jealous or trying to be someone they're not, but we celebrated Messiah and each other's diversity in a kingdom way with worship, dancing, teaching, and fellowship! I heard testimonies from many denominations, and for the first time in my life I not only felt loved but also accepted, and I loved and accepted them too. In Wittenberg I found a beauty I'd never seen before in the colorful tapestry called the Body of Messiah.

CAROLYN HYDE, Messianic Jewish worship leader,
Heart of G-d Ministries, Israel

Friday, November 3—This was going to be a difficult day. I had known it from the early planning stages.[1]

This was the day of repentance to the Anabaptists.

My concern about whether any Anabaptists would come had faded, to be replaced with a new concern. Were the Americans in our midst going to make it through the day?

There was a long talk in German about the atrocities committed against the Anabaptists in the days of Luther. The next talk was even longer. … and also in German. The next talk … well, you get the picture. I was just praying for endurance for my friends from the United States, where our attention span is so often measured in two-minute commercial breaks.

It was around 5:00 PM when Hans-Peter and Verena took the stage. Everyone was exhausted from the talks—not only their length, but also the heaviness of these difficult subjects. Austrian Catholics had drowned Anabaptists, mocking their "adult baptism" as they struggled in the water. The tongues of Anabaptist women had been torn out to prevent them from preaching. In Münster, Germany, the bodies of executed Anabaptist leaders were suspended in cages hung from the bell tower of St. Lambert's Church— and these cages still hang today. Those Anabaptist leaders themselves had led an armed uprising, betraying their principles of nonviolence. Tragedy abounded, and we had heard our fill.

Then repentance began.

Verena invited to the stage all who identified with the Anabaptist faith. Over thirty people came forward—later we learned that a few decided to affirm their Anabaptist roots only at that moment.

---

1 Our large 2017 gathering started on November 1. We had reserved the room in the Best Western for October 31 (see chapter 12), but the group coming was much too large for that room. Some Germans also expressed concern about creating the appearance of an event "in the name of unity" that was in competition with the official celebrations on the actual 500th anniversary. So on October 31, a small group of us gathered in the room that had been reserved in 2010, to watch the official celebrations and pray blessings upon every aspect of them. The next day—providentially All Saints Day—was when we kicked off the main Wittenberg 2017 gathering.

Roman Catholic Cardinal Schönborn of Vienna sent an extraordinary letter, which was read by his archdeacon, Johannes Fichtenbauer:

For putting you into prison and sending your men to the galley ships.

For torture, terrible and obscene harassment against body, health and life.

For taking away the children from the breasts of their mothers.

For burning your leaders at [the] stake …

Please forgive.

I ask forgiveness for not listening to you, to the voice of the Holy Spirit, represented by you and speaking through you. You have challenged our understanding of what is a Christian, what [is the meaning of] baptism, discipleship, martyrdom … and we did not want to hear.

Please forgive.

This has been the past. But it is not undone in the present.

At least, we have continued to sin in the last five decades. We followed the sins of our Catholic fathers. Even when we stopped killing you physically, we still denied your existence, importance, and dignity …

Please forgive.

Holger Bartsch, a Lutheran pastor, named the terrible truth of the Lutheran persecution against the Anabaptists.

I confess the sin of pride and arrogance, which led to rejection, defamation, and devaluing brothers and sisters in Christ from other churches, especially the Anabaptist movements. And I confess the sin of the Lutheran Church forbidding you to preach—we joined in the sin of the political powers, forbidding you to preach the Word of God in public …

Auxiliary Bishop Emeritus Franziskus Eisenbach stood as a leader of the Catholic Church in Germany:

And I personally pray before God and before you, and I ask for forgiveness for every contemptuous, every condemning thought and word that I have spoken with respect to your theology, your teaching, and your way of life.

And so I ask you, Lord Jesus Christ, break this chain of curses that has stretched from this time to now, and has distorted our vision for the beautiful gifts you have given your body through the Anabaptists and through their spiritual descendants who have come out of this source. I break this curse with the sword of the Spirit, and I ask in your grace and your mercy that you take away the consequences of the sins of our fathers in the faith, which have afflicted our church to this very day. And that You restore the gifts and restore the blessings You want to give.

And again Archdeacon Fichtenbauer:

And here is the declaration.

As we have become a terrible curse for you over all these five centuries, here we declare we want to become a blessing to you with the help of God.

Please receive this word as a commitment.

Amen.

The room was silent. The Anabaptists stood still. What was in their minds, in their hearts?

Centuries-old wounds healed in a day, as forgiveness is extended by the Anabaptists gathered on stage. Photo by Ryan and Noleen Thurman. Used with permission.

And then Verena approached to embrace Lloyd Hoover from Pennsylvania … and soon the stage was covered in hugs, in tears, in embraces.

It was absolutely beautiful.

And it was capped by a hope-filled journey into a modern-day Anabaptist community, the Bruderhof—with photos from their lives in the United States, Germany, Paraguay, Australia, South Korea, and the United Kingdom.

And now it was late. Way past dinnertime.

I knew that next on the schedule was the Friday night Shabbat service. I wondered if the weary and hungry gathered there could endure even fifteen more minutes. At least it would be simple and short … or so I thought. And then someone brought to me the plans that the Messianic Jews had drawn up. Multiple musicians, with song after song. A talk on the Torah portion by Richard Harvey. Prayers by Marianna. "This will be at least an hour," I thought.

And I almost made a terrible mistake. I was so close—really for the first time in six years—to exercising my prerogative as leader. I wondered … should I just cut the Shabbat service?

I almost said, "No Shabbat." I am so glad I didn't. I am so glad I trusted my friends.

I am so glad we put ourselves into the hands of our older brother, the Jews. They had graciously received so much repentance through the years. And they knew what to do in response.

The KISI Kids leading the dance! Photo by Ryan and Noleen Thurman. Used with permission.

"Everybody stand up, form a circle, and dance around the room"—came the instructions from Carolyn Hyde as she started a lively Jewish song.

The KISI Kids were already dancing,[1] and as Carolyn gave this instruction the young people grabbed the adults and pulled them into the circle—whether they wanted to or not! Here, at the culminating moment of the entire initiative, it was the youth who led us.

Suddenly Anabaptists in cloth garments with no buttons were arm in arm with the Catholic priests who had just repented to them, whirling by American evangelicals in jeans and T-shirts, flanked by Lutheran nuns and Jewish men in kippahs.

And then these wonderful Austrian Catholic children directed us to turn the single large slow circle into several small tight ones, concentric, moving in alternate directions, dancing, clapping, kicking, reversing. And we danced.

In and out; back and forth; happy faces, linked arms, laughing missteps, graceful gestures. And we kept dancing!

And when the music ended, when the Shabbat service was over, the German royalty produced grilled meat, warm rolls, and glasses of award-winning white wine—seemingly from nowhere—and we feasted together breathlessly, all wondering—what just happened?

Repentance—Joy.

Only in Jesus can these two movements of the human heart—one a dirge, one a wedding—join into garlands for ashes, oil for mourning, and a garment of praise for a heavy spirit. "Sorrow may last for the night ... but joy comes in the morning!"

I am confident that nobody who was there that night will ever forget it. Even as I write these words well over two years later, I just received this description in an email:

It was one of the closest glimpses of heaven on earth I've seen.

---

1 The KISI Kids are an Austrian children's singing group who showed up in force in 2017. Mostly Catholics, but also including Protestants and Messianic Jews—they were absolutely wonderful! For more information about them, see https://www.kisi.org/en/.

Richard and Marianna celebrating Shabbat. Photo by Ryan and Noleen Thurman.
Used with permission.

There is a beautiful photograph from that evening of Richard Harvey and Marianna Gol that recalls for me the words that Richard had published earlier that year:

> I'm looking for a Jewish circle dance to break out in heaven and catch everyone up in its swirling excitement. So let's get dancing today! I want to see this wherever the anniversary of Luther is celebrated, so that Jews, Germans, and Jewish believers in Jesus can dance together. Only then will Luther's dream of the kingdom of God on earth be established.[2]

These words were indeed prophetic. May they continue to prophesy to the people of God around the world!

Use the QR code or visit **https://bit.ly/w17ch24** to explore more pictures and additional material for this chapter, including a video with highlights from the day of repentance and joyful dancing.

---

2 *Luther and the Jews*, 124. See also chapter 16.

Part V

Sabbath and New Life

Chapter 25

The Beauty of Completability

Wittenberg 2017. The 500th anniversary of the Reformation was a fitting time to pray for God's Spirit to bring forth a Christ-glorifying unity. I joined many friends and leaders, some I'd known for years, in a unique prayer event held in Wittenberg, Germany, during the first five days of November. The times of prayer were wonderful. But the signs and reports of unity were what I found most encouraging. God is doing great things in our day!

STEVEN HAWTHORNE, PhD, Hope Chapel (Protestant / nondenominational), editor of *Perspectives on the World Christian Movement*, author of *Seek God for the City*, Austin, Texas USA

I did not attend this year's conference, but I followed up on it from afar. I love what you do, and the spirit you carry with you, and the centrality of God and the message he has burned on your hearts. Powerful, simple, refreshing.

And I love the idea of completability. It ministers deeply to me.

Good job, faithful servants. We say in Hebrew: "Kol HaKavod" and "Ko Le-hai." It is well respected and honored, and it brings forth life.

ORNA GRINMAN, Messianic Jew, Ot OoMofet Ministries, Israel

Person after person, thrilled by the experience of reconciliation and unity, came up to me with this question—"So, when's the next meeting?"

They were always surprised by my answer. This had been a question that our leadership team had been considering for several years. We usually phrased it like this:

"Is the gathering in 2017 an ending? … or a beginning?"

I usually advocated for it being an ending. My natural gifting is to start things, not continue or maintain them. The idea of an unbounded Wittenberg 2017 sounded wearying.

Many voices were on the other side. Momentum continued to grow from meeting to meeting, and surely that would continue after 2017. We had formed a unique leadership team across the Atlantic that prioritized unity over quick, or even effective, decision-making. Our Principles were powerful,[1] our Historical Conclusions were incisive,[2] and our prayer models had proven workable in both Catholic and Protestant contexts. We had developed friendships and connections on three continents. So many volunteers had invested their time and talents: Gaby Schubert and Caroline Owens in intercession; John Martin in translation; Franz Rathmair and Jo Hoffman in media; John Michael Wall in art; and the list could go on and on. Surely these resources should not be lightly set aside.

After the meeting in 2016 had concluded, we gathered as a leadership team in an "upper room"—the library of the Leucorea. The purpose was to determine which direction to take, as we planned the 2017 gathering. For a while, we went back and forth, with no clear consensus. Then Amy wisely encouraged us: "We need to hear from God. Let's take ten minutes, be silent before the Lord, and listen in our hearts." And so we did.

Ten minutes later, we began to share around the circle of chairs. Somehow, unity came. It was miraculous—a true work of the Spirit.

We would end the initiative after the 2017 gathering.

This decision produced various reactions and emotions among us.

For me and some others, this was a tremendous relief! It made the 500 days of planning ahead of us, with the culminating meeting, feel exciting instead of draining. We would do it—then we would be done. Whew.

Others were sad—already anticipating the loss of regular relational touch-points, as our leadership team disbanded.

Many had mixed emotions.

But we all recognized that we had heard from God.

We did not announce this conclusion publicly before the final gathering in 2017. So those who asked me about the next meeting were always surprised when I replied:

---

1 See appendix 1, The Wittenberg 2017 Principles.
2 See appendix 2, Historical Conclusions about the Reformation.

"There isn't a next meeting. This is the last one."

"What? Why?" was the invariable response.

"Wait until Sunday. We'll explain it then."

Dr. Hawthorne (*left*) and Prince Michael Salm (*right*) pray over me and Amy on the last day of the gathering. Photo by Ryan and Noleen Thurman. Used with permission.

Sunday was the last session of our final gathering. When that day arrived, there was still a buzz in the room from the amazing KISI Kids musical Ruth the night before. I walked slowly forward to the podium. Scanning the room for one face in particular, I was happy when I saw that my friend Dr. Steve Hawthorne was in his seat.

Steve edits the well-known *Perspectives* missions course, which is taught around the world. He and his wife, Barbara, also sit in the pew directly behind our family at Hope Chapel in Austin. I had learned the heart of what I was about to say from Steve a decade earlier, and I was very happy to be able to publicly honor him that day as an important mentor.

My talk was entitled "The Beauty of Completability."

The initiative's ending is as important as its beginning.

The power of many initiatives has been diminished because they didn't end when God had finished his work. Leaders naturally want to build on momentum. Organizations that have been constructed have inertia. But the key ingredient is God's anointing. If that is lifted, the movement will get more and more difficult, until it simply peters out, at best, or at worst self-destructs, damaging many people.

What is the biblical basis for this?

We have been praying through John 17 for the last four days. Let's look at what Jesus says about his own ministry in John 17:4: "I have brought you glory on earth by finishing the work you gave me to do."

This is an amazing statement. Jesus knew the task that God gave him. He knew that it was a completable task. And he knew that he had completed the task. I call this "the beauty of completability."

Jesus was the Son of God. His Father did not give him unending work to do. This is remarkable! The Son of God! ... and his assignment was limited and completable!

How much more so do we need limited and completable tasks?

This was a revelation our leadership team had come to in that upper room in 2016. Not even Jesus had an open-ended assignment! We could follow in our Master's footsteps and be content to end Wittenberg 2017 after the final meeting.

We would then be able to say, with Jesus:

We have brought you glory on the earth by finishing the work you gave us to do.

The final leadership meeting, to celebrate the completion of the Wittenberg 2017 initiative. Photo by Thomas Cogdell.

And this is what we said on Sunday afternoon, as the international council of Wittenberg 2017 settled down for one last time around one last table. We celebrated what God had done, expressed our gratitude to him, and reaffirmed our love for each other.

Wittenberg 2017 had ended, Hallelujah!

Wittenberg 2017 had ended well, Hallelujah! Hallelujah!

But ending Wittenberg 2017 did not mean the end of our relationships with each other—Hallelujah! Hallelujah! Hallelujah!

 Use the QR code or visit **https://bit.ly/w17ch25** to explore more pictures and additional material for this chapter, including how an Eastern Orthodox priest from Istanbul appeared in Wittenberg.

Chapter 26

"Unless a Seed Falls
into the Ground"

We miss the annual meetings, the time spent together in Christian love, and we are very pleased with the deep relationships with friends that arose through Wittenberg 2017. Here are some examples of what came out of it for us:

- *A new stream of blessing was unleashed for our marriage and for our larger family. We reaped the fruits since all of our grown children, led by the Holy Spirit, started great new initiatives, recognized their own talents, and put them to use for the glory of God.*
- *Renewed and deep engagement in the history of the Reformation. Together with the participants in the movement, we became aware of unresolved grievances that had to be brought to light.*
- *In our work with the body of Christ, together with the Messianic Jews, we experienced new beginnings, friendships, and deep connection with Israel.*
- *We got to experience reconciliation of the Amish and Mennonite streams with the traditional churches and saw the continuation of that reconciliation in the subsequent visit to the Catholic Congress in Münster in 2018, where the great blessing continued to flow.*

PRINCE MICHAEL and PRINCESS PHILIPPA SALM, Roman Catholic (Michael) / Evangelical Lutheran (Philippa), Walhausen, Germany

The Wittenberg 2017 initiative was one of the most meaningful, enriching, and fruitful ministries I have ever been involved in. It was born in the hearts of Christian friends, Catholic and Protestant, who had long grieved historic divisions between those who self-identify as followers of Jesus. How to respond meaningfully and redemptively? While honoring our spiritual forefathers and mothers, we openly and painfully identified with their wrongs. "Both we and our fathers have sinned" (Ps. 106:6a). We expressed deep sadness. Confession and repentance brought forth responses of forgiveness and reconciliation. Soon the fellowship was growing, and representatives from other traditions were joining. During our closing service, we "commissioned" attendees to go and catalyze new initiatives of reconciliation in their own contexts.

That service was led by seven clergy, representing Messianic Jews, Eastern Orthodox, Roman Catholics, German Lutherans, Anabaptists, Anglicans, and nondenominational Protestants.[1] Soli Deo Gloria!

GEORGE MILEY, Anglican priest, pioneer of the Logos and Doulos ship ministry for Operation Mobilization, co-founder of Antioch Network, co-founder of Quellen, Phoenix, Arizona USA

Ending Wittenberg 2017 did not finish our work of reconciliation. In so many ways, it is just beginning to unfold.

When Jesus was faced with the cross, he spoke a profound word: "… unless a grain of wheat falls into the earth and dies, it remains alone; but if it dies, it bears much fruit" (John 12:24; ESV). This was the other scripture, along with John 17:4, that we had heard as a leadership team back in 2016. We understood that the two scriptures were to work together. We were to complete what God had called us to do by ending the Wittenberg 2017 initiative. This would be like the seed that falls into the ground and dies.

But, then … God would do what only he can do. He would bring forth fruit. Life from death! And it is happening.

Here are five short stories of new works that are springing forth, born by the power of God out of the seed that was Wittenberg 2017.

The Trinational Triangle

Jochen Debus was among the first German Lutheran pastors to become involved in Wittenberg 2017. Jochen's wife, Miriam, contributed her lovely flute-playing to our worship times in many of the meetings. When I asked them for a memory for this book, Miriam sent this story—which I had not previously heard.

One event stands out among many experiences. In Wittenberg in 2016, I felt a great burden resting on me for the guilt of my ancestors at the border known as the "Trinational Triangle"—where Germany, Switzerland, and France meet. Many Jews fled across the natural border called the "Eiserne Hand" (iron hand), from Lörrach to Riehen. But the police in Riehen often sent the Jews back to Nazi-occupied France, which meant a certain death.

Now, I am a Swiss citizen living in Germany on this same border. God put the burden of this border, which had been deadly to Jews, on me. But he also gave me the charge and the ability to release freedom, forgiveness, and restoration.

---

1 See the beginning of chapter 1 for a picture of this service.

I joined Benjamin Berger from Israel in the working group and asked him as a vicarious representative for my region for forgiveness, for deliverance and restoration in this border region. He was quite willing to do this because he had already been doing it for some time. He also told everyone how his grandparents had fled across this border and how the police had deported them to France, to certain death.

And what has been the fruit of his reconciliation and forgiveness? For two years now, people from all sides of the border and all Christian denominations have been meeting in Riehen for revival meetings. "Awakening Basel" has come into being. Prayer meetings are being held and prayer rooms opened in churches and houses across the borders of these countries. Children of God are meeting with a longing in their hearts to live in unity.

This partnership between Miriam and Benjamin beautifully demonstrates how relationships formed in the Wittenberg 2017 meetings have not ended, but are deepening and widening.

Two Movies from Philadelphia

Starting in 2013, I formed a friendship with John Armstrong. John is a scholar in the United States with a huge heart for the unity of the body of Christ—somewhat unusual for a leader in the Reformed Evangelical tradition.

> "I can't come, but did I tell you that I'm sending a film crew?"

Throughout 2017, John and I kept in touch. I called him less than a month before the gathering, hoping he might be able to attend, and John surprised me with these words: "I can't come, but did I tell you that I'm sending a film crew?"

When a few weeks later I met the film crew of two—David and Kathi Peters from Philadelphia—I was nervous. Would they inject themselves into the meeting in an inappropriate way? Would they demand special lighting setups? Would they interrupt the flow of prayer to fasten special microphones on the leaders' shirts? David and Kathi immediately set me at ease. I was amazed at how unobtrusive they could be—blending in with the gathering, two worshippers who happened to be holding cameras.

And then, when I saw the finished product, I was amazed again. Looking at the footage, anyone would guess there was a large film crew orchestrating lighting and sound throughout. How did they do it? Their trade secret, I guess!

But the best part was—David and Kathi "got it." They themselves had suffered from hostility in the body of Christ. They longed for reconciliation and unity. They understood our hearts. They recognized the treasures in those who had come to Wittenberg and took the time to interview so many of them. Then they followed up afterward—visiting the Salms in Germany again and coming to Texas to have more in-depth discussions with Amy and me.

Kathi and David Peters came to Texas to film additional interviews with Amy and me at Christ the Reconciler. Photo by Thomas Cogdell.

In 2020, they released what we believe to be the first full-length documentary focused on unity and reconciliation in the body of Christ—a film named *One: Following Jesus' Call for Unity*. I was surprised to find the first narrative in the film is Wittenberg 2017! The remainder of the film has story after story, and interspersed throughout is commentary from leading thinkers in the global church—N. T. Wright, Father Robert Barron, Richard Harvey, and many others.

David and Kathi worked closely with John Armstrong's group called *The Initiative*. They also produced a related film focused on "interchurch marriage." Called *Will Faith Do Us Part?*, it tells the stories of three Protestant–Catholic marriages. These marriages open a window into the pain caused by divisions in the body of Christ. They also speak to the hope of love triumphing over hostility. Two of the three marriages David and Kathi filmed were of couples they met in Wittenberg—Amy and me, and Prince Michael and Princess Philippa Salm.

What will be the impact of these two unique films? How many will see them and be challenged to care about what Jesus cares about—the oneness of his followers? How many other films and multimedia projects about reconciliation and unity in the body of Christ will be inspired by these first two?

Only God knows ...

The Münster Cages

The surprises of the Holy Spirit continue. In the research for the writing of this book, I reached out to Lloyd Hoover, an Anabaptist leader from Pennsylvania who was present at the repentance service in 2017.

Lloyd's Anabaptist ancestral roots stretch back generations to Reformation times and include eight martyrs. He has served as a Mennonite bishop for the last twenty-five years, and for the last twenty he has served on an Anabaptist mission to see healing and reconciliation regarding this troubled history. Over those two decades, the Spirit highlighted one story in particular.

The terrible cages hanging high on St. Lambert's in Münster. Photo by David and Kathi Peters. Used with permission.

In the 1530s, some German Anabaptists revolted and took over the town of Münster. They committed many atrocities, and in turn atrocities were revisited upon them. The Catholic bishop Franz von Waldeck led an army to retake the city, and Anabaptist leaders were executed. To make an example, von Waldeck ordered the bodies of three leaders suspended in open cages that swung from the church in the center of the city. The bones have long since fallen out, but the cages hang there to this day.

In 2001, the group of Mennonite leaders that Lloyd was part of identified Münster as a key point of Anabaptist repentance. Why? Because it was the source of a widespread resistance to the Holy Spirit. Anabaptists feared falling prey to the excesses of the Münster leaders, so they kept a tight hold on the reins. This tight hold, the Mennonite leaders now felt, had truly hampered the Anabaptists through the centuries. They wanted this closed spirit to be done away with … but how?

By 2017, Lloyd recounted to me, the attempt to seek reconciliation regarding Münster had been at a standstill for a decade. But when he arrived in Wittenberg, he was surprised to find that Prince Michael Salm and his wife, Princess Philippa, were also present. Lloyd had given Prince Michael a prophetic word ten years previously, in 2007, that he was the one who held the key to open the Münster door for healing. And here was Prince Michael! And with him Princess Philippa—a descendant of the very same von Waldeck family.

"Let's have breakfast," Lloyd proposed.

As they talked, they realized that in just a few months Münster would be the site of the 2018 Kirchentag (Church day). Thousands of German Catholics would descend on the city. Through the influence of the Salms, a service of repentance and reconciliation was quickly planned for St. Lambert's Church. With the cages still dangling outside, the Catholics repented for the horrific vengeance perpetrated by their forefathers all those centuries ago. The Anabaptists expressed remorse for the acts committed by their ancestors as well, during the rebellion. Both sides offered forgiveness to each other and made new commitments to unity and cooperation.[2]

Are you as amazed as I am at the sovereignty of God? In 2007, seemingly unrelated events were in motion in Texas and Pennsylvania that no human being could have imagined would converge a decade later in Germany. The years in between were filled with ordinary actions of obedience, mistakes, waiting, trusting, and preparation. Then God said, "Now!"—and the fullness-of-time moment arrived.

The Cardinal's Offer

On Saturday morning during the 2017 gathering, John Dawson called Ben Girod up to the podium.

A distinguished and long-standing Amish leader from Montana, Ben had been appointed by the Anabaptists to respond to the repentance of the previous day. Ben's words

The Amish leader Ben Girod was asked by John Dawson to address the gathering the day after repentance toward the Anabaptists. Photo by Franz Rathmair. Used with permission.

---

2 Because the filmmakers David and Kathi Peters had met the Salms in Wittenberg, they also were invited to the Münster reconciliation. Beautiful footage from this event found its way into both of their films.

provided a capstone to the joy of repentance from Friday. He spoke as a father, releasing spiritual children to fully pursue God's purposes. Then he directly addressed the history of the Anabaptists in Europe:

> *The Anabaptists that gave their lives on European soil, their blood is crying out for this moment, their blood is crying out for healing and for restoration, that we find what they couldn't find, that we accomplish what they couldn't accomplish, and that is, coming together in one heart, and one mind, and one spirit.*

One dimension of what Ben Girod spoke of—perhaps prophesied is a better word—has since unfolded in Austria. The following account was sent to me by Johannes Fichtenbauer, archdeacon of Vienna and ecumenical advisor to Cardinal Christoph Schönborn, who had sent the letter of repentance to be read by Johannes in Wittenberg. That letter had ended by expressing hope for the opportunity to make restitution, setting right the wrongs of the past. Johannes's words show how the Cardinal's offer to aid the Anabaptists became a reality.

> *My highlight during the Wittenberg gathering was the evening when a group of representatives from the historic churches asked all the present Anabaptist brothers and sisters for forgiveness for the sins that the Catholics, Lutherans, and Reformed committed against them. Tears were running and we hardly were able to speak. Everyone felt the heaviness of God's presence in the hall. This was a unique moment of authentic representative confession, encounter, and reconciliation.*

> *Would it be possible to make this spiritual act of reconciliation even more concrete by living out brotherhood and cooperation on a day-to-day basis with Catholic and Protestant believers, the former enemies?*

> *As a result of this evening, a year later we heard from a married couple from the Bruderhof in England, Kim and Ulrike Comer, who had been sent by their community as "spies" into Austria to check out the possibilities of establishing a Bruderhof community in this former "enemy-land." Kim and Ulrike met with the delegates of the Round Table, the largest platform for Christian unity in Austria. Immediately Kim and Ulrike were of one heart and soul with me and the other Round Table members. A pioneering team was created to help them to find the best possible place for a new Bruderhof settlement.*

> *Deeply touched, I reported to the Cardinal of Vienna, Christoph Schönborn, about all these developments. The Cardinal was excited from the first moment. He had previously met the grandson of the*

Bruderhof's founder in the 1990s and had kept an eye on them ever since. Now the opportunity arose to set an example for reconciliation for the whole Christian world.

Graciously the Cardinal offered his connection to an old Dominican monastery in a village called Retz, ninety minutes north of Vienna. The building seemed to be a good place for the initial group of forty people. When the international Bruderhof elders came to visit the old monastery, there was great conviction among them that God had selected this place for them.

Already in the autumn of 2019 the first families of this new Bruderhof community had moved into the houses in Retz. Further studies documented that exactly this area where the monastery was located was one of the hot spots where the Hutterites fled to in the 1500s by the thousands, only to be persecuted. This new Bruderhof home is becoming a very concrete place of reconciliation between the Catholic Church and the Hutterite heritage. Former enemies have turned into allies for the Kingdom.

The former convent outside Vienna that has become the new home for the Bruderhof in Austria.
Photo by Andrew Zimmerman. Used with permission.

In 2021, with the Cardinal's assistance, the Bruderhof purchased and began to move into a former convent near Vienna, which is becoming the permanent Austrian home for their community. Martin Johnson, with whom I had that first conversation while in the Houston Zoo, wrote to tell me about it, ending with this:

[The] Wittenberg Conference … a very historic event with fruits still coming.

What Are Amy and Thomas Doing Now?

This story briefly picks up some of the threads left hanging earlier in the book, about the Austin House of Prayer. Chapter 3 describes how I started AHOP, and chapter 8 describes how I repented of many compulsive aspects of leadership that were sown into AHOP from the beginning. AHOP had to be *unformed*, in order to be *reconstituted* into what God had in mind all along. That process took about ten years, culminating in 2015 when we changed the ministry's name from AHOP to Christ the Reconciler (CTR). This name change rightly locates both the motivation and the means for reconciliation in Jesus.

After making this name change, we put the development of CTR mostly on hold for Wittenberg.

This was a divinely ordered "pause."

In the buildup for 2017, I learned of the Anabaptists. I discovered that the wonderfully diverse groups who identify with this stream of the body of Christ share one foundational principle: "living out the Sermon on the Mount." I loved this phrase! It was so simple, yet so profound. When I heard it, I immediately understood what they were about; but I also grasped the challenge of actually doing it.

As we gathered for the 500th anniversary, this phrase began to meld together with the idea of praying John 17. I began to wonder: What would it be like to *live out John 17?*

I brought this question to Amy, then Phillip and Caroline, and then we introduced it to the wider CTR community. Together, we discerned that God was inviting our small group of Protestants and Catholics in central Texas to dive into this deep question.

And this is what we are doing, soberly but with our whole hearts.

Learning to live out John 17.

Because … since 2017, the church in America has fractured into polarized camps of increasing hostility.

Is unity through repentance possible in the United States?

As we have learned from our dear brothers and sisters in Europe—indeed it is.

It is the only way forward.

These have been just a few stories of new works that are springing forth. Perhaps yours is the next one?

Please take a minute, quiet your heart, and read out loud what Paul wrote in 2 Corinthians 5:18, truly owning it as your calling:

> All this is from God, who reconciled us to himself through Christ and gave us the ministry of reconciliation.

Amen.

Maranatha!

Come quickly, Lord Jesus …

Use the QR code or visit **https://bit.ly/w17ch26** to explore more pictures and additional material for this chapter, including more stories of fruitfulness springing forth from Wittenberg 2017.

Afterword

By Hanna Zack Miley

While this book was still in progress, Thomas asked me to end it with a benediction. His request made me think back on the many years we traveled together—a band of ordinary disciples called from the divided body of Christ. It also called me to reflect on how my own personal journey of reconciliation prepared the way for this new work of God.

On the evening of July 24, 1939, my German Jewish parents stood with tears in their eyes as I clambered up steep steps to a train at the Köln Hauptbahnhof (the main train station in Cologne, Germany). We had moved from our idyllic village of Gemünd to the city of Köln after *Kristallnacht*—the night on which Jewish synagogues and businesses throughout Germany had been vandalized or completely destroyed. That was the tipping point that drove my parents to secure a priceless place for me on the Kindertransport—a rescue effort that saved the lives of 10,000 Jewish children from Germany, Austria, Czechoslovakia, and Poland.

I didn't realize that moment would be our last glimpse of each other. In one fateful day, I lost my language, my culture, my religion, and the love of my family. I was taken to England and placed in the home of a British family that wanted to help but had no awareness of Jewish ways or traditions.

Britain was at war. Fear of invasion was pervasive, and in the early 1940s the way to deal with trauma was to suck it up. I can remember hearing, "What a lucky girl you are!" My teenage years were fraught with anger and hatred toward Germans. Deep down I felt my parents had abandoned me.

I didn't know where to go with all my darkness. I was coming to the end of coping when I encountered the living Jesus. I learned for the first time that I could lift up the ugly weight of wrongness I was carrying to Jesus, hanging on the cross.

That was the beginning of my healing journey. I left my job as a teacher and spent the next several decades in Christian ministry, traveling the world to share the gospel message of hope and forgiveness. And still the Lord was working in me. To my surprise, he led me back to Germany when I was sixty years old.

It is one thing to forgive from the safety of distance, but something else to go back to the places where my parents and I had been wronged, to begin to forgive amid the physical scenes of abuse, injustice, and death. I experienced both grief and healing power released when I joined with other dear friends to pray at these painful sites.

I experienced a similarly profound work of God during our journey with Wittenberg 2017, as we made pilgrimage to places where followers of Jesus had accused, excommunicated, and even killed one another.

There are many wounds in the body of Messiah. Some of those wounds are personal; others are historical. If we are willing, we can choose not to ignore the great pain these wounds cause to God, and to ourselves. This is the first step.

My prayer is that each of us will encounter Jesus, hanging on the cross, and find healing in his mercy.

I will close by praying Aaron's blessing over us all: those who traveled together to Wittenberg; and especially you, the reader, because you have now also entered into that journey.

> The Lord bless you and keep you; the Lord make his face shine upon you, and be gracious to you; the Lord lift up His countenance upon you, and give you peace. (Num 6:24–26; NKJV)

HANNA ZACK MILEY
Phoenix, AZ
December 2021

 Use the QR code or visit **https://bit.ly/w17apx3hzm** to get to know Hanna Miley better.

Appendix 1: The Wittenberg 2017 Principles

I wrote the first draft of the Wittenberg 2017 Principles while flying across the Pacific Ocean in 2010, on my way to South Korea for an Athens Group project.

1. The irresistible purpose of Jesus is to return to a united Church universal.
2. The current reality is that the Church universal is divided—in heart, purpose, thinking, and organizational structures.
3. Division weakens the Church universal.
4. The Church universal should feel the pain of her divisions and grieve them.
5. The Church universal should pray for reconciliation and unity.

These principles were both expanded and refined by the leadership team. Reading them out loud together each time we met grounded our gatherings in a unified purpose.

 Use the QR code or visit **https://bit.ly/w17apx1** to read the fully expanded version of the Principles, as well as access PDFs in German and other languages.

Appendix 2:
Historical Conclusions about the Reformation

The Historical Conclusions were compiled between the 2015 and 2016 gatherings.

1. We honor Martin Luther as a prophet sent by God to Luther's own church, the Roman Catholic Church.
2. We lament that Luther's prophetic message was not correctly considered or responded to by his apostolic authorities.

3. We grieve the subsequent shared history of hostility—and ask the Holy Spirit to embolden us to identify with our forefathers, repent for their attitudes and actions that were not godly, forgive, and where appropriate make restitution.

4. We believe that Catholics and Protestants can and should jointly commemorate the 500th anniversary of the Reformation.

5. We propose that Catholics and Protestants—indeed all followers of Jesus—seize the opportunity to pray John 17 with Jesus on the occasion of this historic anniversary.

6. We believe that in preparation for Jesus's return, the Holy Spirit will move again as Malachi prophesied, "turning the hearts of the fathers to the children and the children to their fathers."

As with the Principles, the leadership team expanded each of these conclusions to unfold the evidence for and implications of each one.

Use the QR code or visit **https://bit.ly/w17apx2** to read the fully expanded version of the Historical Conclusions.

Appendix 3:
Biographical Sketches by Amy Cogdell

In 2018, Amy wrote a series of lovely blog posts, in which she recorded some of her memories and impressions of key leaders of Wittenberg 2017. Amy is a much better writer than I am!

Use the QR code or visit **https://bit.ly/w17apx3langs** to get to know Hans-Peter and Verena Lang better.

Use the QR code or visit **https://bit.ly/w17apx3gm** to get to know George Miley better.

 Use the QR code or visit **https://bit.ly/w17apx3hzm** to get to know Hanna Miley better.

Use the QR code or visit **https://bit.ly/w17apx3srj** to get to know Sister Joela Krüger better.

 Use the QR code or visit **https://bit.ly/w17apx3fr** to get to know Auxiliary Bishop Emeritus Franziskus Eisenbach better.

Appendix 4:
Wittenberg 2017 as One Pattern for Leadership of a Reconciliation Initiative

George Miley gave permission to adopt a paper he had written, called *Development of a Work of God: Principles.*[1] The Wittenberg 2017 initiative beautifully illustrates the pattern George outlined.

1 – God Initiates the Reconciliation Initiative

2 – God Chooses a Leader

3 – God Draws Others into the Vision

4 – God Creates an Intercessory Covering

5 – God Forms a Mutually Submitted Leadership Team

---

1 This paper is article 106 of a compilation by George, Hanna, and some friends entitled *Ancient Wells: Foundations for Christian Worship, Theology and Formation.* As of the writing of this book, *Ancient Wells* remains unpublished.

6 – God Faithfully Shepherds the Initiative through Stages of Growth

7 – God Calls Forth Specific, Meaningful Actions of Reconciliation

8 – God Begins Other Works while Ending the Initiative

Our hope in publishing this paper as an appendix is to provide guidance for potential future reconciliation initiatives—with the understanding, of course, that each initiative is unique and will experience its own "surprises of the Spirit."

 Use the QR code or visit **https://bit.ly/w17apx4** to read the full paper, *Wittenberg 2017 as One Pattern for Leadership of a Reconciliation Initiative.*

Appendix 5: Identificational Repentance

Early in the Wittenberg 2017 initiative, Hans-Peter and Verena Lang introduced a short paper by Helmut Eiwen. The paper provided a brief theological foundation for "identificational repentance." John Martin translated it into English, and we made it available to everyone who registered for each of the annual gatherings leading up to 2017, so that we would all be "on the same page" regarding this important topic.

 Use the QR code or visit **https://bit.ly/w17apx5** to read Helmut Eiwen's paper on *Identificational Repentance.*

Appendix 6:
A Lutheran Pastor Reflects on Rome,
by Hans Scholz

After the Rome gathering, Hans Scholz recorded some reflections in an article for a German Lutheran newsletter. He has graciously extended permission for us to reprint his article. The article, written in German, was translated into English by John Martin.

Use the QR code or visit **https://bit.ly/w17apx6** to read Hans Scholz's article.

Appendix 7: Judensau Lament

Chapter 19 describes how Richard Harvey composed his lament when sitting below the Wittenberg Judensau in 2016. After that gathering, the words of the lament were set to music by Richard's friend Alexander Dietze.

Use the QR code or visit **https://bit.ly/w17apx7** to read Richard's lament, listen to Alexander's song, and view a video that incorporates portions of both.

Acknowledgments

If you've made it this far, to the very end of the book, you certainly realize that this story would not exist but for so many people other than myself. I was just along for the ride!

The same is true of writing this book to tell the story of Wittenberg 2017.

In some instances, in this book, when a recording or direct source was not available, I recreated or summarized statements, conversations, teachings, and dialogue from my memory. I ask forgiveness in advance for any omissions or misstatements, which hopefully are not serious. In one instance, I have changed the name of an individual to protect her privacy.

See **https://www.drandrewjackson.com/publications/** for more about the IEB, a unique translation of the New Testament used in this book, written especially for those reading the Bible for the first time, and people who speak English as a second language.

Rather than attempting to list briefly everyone to whom I owe a happy debt of gratitude here, I have created a web page to be able to more fully express my thankfulness.

 Use the QR code or visit **https://bit.ly/w17thanks** to read the Acknowledgments.